AF556142

NEXT IN LINE

'*Next in Line* offers an honest, practical and timely perspective on what it truly means for a young professional to step into a family business. Avishkar brings together personal experiences, thoughtful reflections, and clear, actionable insights that are often missing from mainstream business literature.

'The book captures the realities of leadership, responsibility and modernizing legacy systems with refreshing clarity. It will be especially valuable for next-generation leaders navigating both opportunity and expectation while shaping the future of their family enterprises.'

—Sanjam Gupta
Founder, Maritime SheEO

'I first met Avishkar in 2022 at the FFFAI (Federation of Freight Forwarders' Association of India) National Convention in Chennai. Even then, I was impressed by his thinking, particularly his thought processes for someone so young. His trajectory and journey in the industry have been very different from mine.

'The very fact that Avishkar has written this book speaks volumes about his mental strength, aptitude and, most importantly, his intelligence. To me, this book is a unique combination of work therapy, a practical work guide and a brilliant way to take your company to the next level, without spending lakhs on business coaches.

'My own training, by today's standards, would be called a boot camp. Today's youngsters, or even those from a generation or two ago, would probably not be able to endure it. It would fail spectacularly today, but it made me who I am, so I have no regrets. Reading Avishkar's book felt, honestly, like going back to business school. It becomes crystal clear why attending a B-school helps: your thinking, methods, and systems are fundamentally different.

'Avishkar has a bright future and the potential to become a great leader and logistician. This book is a clear demonstration of that. It is a must-read, as every reader will find at least one valuable idea or practice that they can implement in their own organization.

'It's been an eye-opener for me on several aspects.'

—Chaitaly Mehta
Director, EKF Global Logistics Pvt Ltd

'What impressed me most is that the book not only discusses challenges and solutions specific to family businesses but also beautifully connects them with broader principles of organizational management. Throughout the chapters, general management concepts are seamlessly integrated with real-life challenges faced by individuals entering and growing within a family business environment.

'In most family businesses, one joins what is essentially a well-oiled machine, not a startup. Much of the learning happens through observation, because no one explicitly tells you what to do.

'Grandfathers, fathers and uncles rarely sit down to formally teach management—they simply lived it, and the next generation absorbs it through experience.

'The book highlights a powerful truth: in a family business, "everyone knows how to look, but not everyone knows how to see". This perspective shapes how challenges must be approached and reinforces the importance of adhering to the company's guiding principles and values. A family business is not merely a business—it is a legacy built on people, purpose and possibilities.

'Your work reflects deep clarity, practical wisdom and a strong foundation in management thought. Truly, you are Kolkata's Peter Drucker.'

—S. Padmanabhan
Director, Sattva Logistics Group

'I am very happy that, through this book, Avishkar is guiding the next generation of family business members. Everyone must understand the vision and mission of their family business, and how the next generation is steering the organization towards a bright future built on strong fundamentals, ethics and sound management principles.

'The book helps youngsters realize that they should not view their legacy business as a burden, but rather approach it with enthusiasm to achieve organizational goals and targets.

'I sincerely hope this book becomes a guiding light for the next generation in family businesses.'

—G. Sambasiva Rao
Managing Director, Sravan Shipping Services Pvt Ltd

NEXT IN LINE

A Youngster's Guide to Indian Family Business

AVISHKAR SRIVASTAVA

RUPA

Published by
Rupa Publications India Pvt. Ltd 2026
161-B/4, Gulmohar House,
Yusuf Sarai Community Centre,
New Delhi 110049

Sales centres
Bengaluru Chennai
Hyderabad Kolkata Mumbai

P-ISBN: 978-93-5352-180-6
E-ISBN: 978-93-5352-306-0

First impression 2026

10 9 8 7 6 5 4 3 2 1

Printed in India

Contents

Foreword

Before I begin, it is important to briefly reflect on how Avishkar's grandfather founded The PDP Group®, which has today grown into one of the best-known and largest logistics groups in eastern India. The organization was further nurtured, expanded and strengthened by his father, Shri Pramod Kumar Srivastava, my good friend. It is indeed heartening to note that Avishkar chose to join the family business and carry forward this rich legacy.

Avishkar rightly points out that more than 80 per cent of Indian companies are family-owned, and this trend is not unique to India. In Europe, over 60 per cent of businesses are family-owned, and more than 60 per cent of the US GDP is generated by family enterprises. Yet, very few management books deal specifically with the nuances of family businesses in the Indian context, especially within the MSME sector.

What makes Avishkar's book truly distinctive is that it is written by someone who joined his own family business over a decade ago, experienced its intricacies first-hand, and has now created a practical handbook of dos and don'ts for youngsters who are either joining, or planning to join, their family businesses. This is what lends the book both credibility and authenticity.

Most family businesses in India—particularly MSMEs—

have traditionally depended heavily on the founder or one key individual for guidance and operations. However, in today's world, growth is impossible without industry knowledge, digitalization, structured processes, robust systems and a professional governance model. It is commendable that this realization dawned on Avishkar early, prompting him to take decisive steps to transform the organization.

His practice of addressing his father and mother as 'Sir' and 'Ma'am' in the office is both interesting and symbolic. It clearly separates professional and personal roles, while strengthening workplace discipline.

He emphasizes that a company cannot focus only on revenue, profit and growth; it must also build the right culture for long-term sustainability. His efforts have not only contributed to the rapid growth of the organization but have also brought national recognition, including the award for Best Practices in Employee Value Proposition.

He explains that the ultimate aim must be to create a workplace culture that is employee-friendly, impartial, knowledge-driven, customer-focused and growth-oriented. He also highlights the importance of employee feedback. I found his concept of the SMART framework for workplace culture particularly insightful—Specific, Measurable, Achievable, Realistic and Timely.

Avishkar further stresses the importance of a clearly defined vision and mission, shared not just with promoters but across every level of the organization. Communication is emphasized repeatedly, especially with drivers, who play a crucial role in the logistics industry.

One of the most commendable achievements of The PDP Group has been its commitment to HR professionalism. Recruitment, which was once informal and reference-based, is now conducted through structured advertisements, interviews and psychometric assessments. Performance appraisals have been upgraded, incorporating 360-degree feedback and data-driven evaluation.

Avishkar writes candidly about difficult HR situations, such as dealing with senior, long-serving employees who negatively impact the work environment. He rightly emphasizes that such matters must be handled professionally: by giving individuals opportunities to improve and, if necessary, taking tough decisions in the long-term interest of the organization.

Another significant challenge in family businesses is the generation gap. The younger generation often brings fresh ideas but struggles to convince senior members. They can either continue established practices or step outside their comfort zone to transform the business. Avishkar explains this dynamic with honesty and humility, emphasizing that respect for experience and clarity of purpose must go hand in hand.

His insights reminded me of my own early career, when I joined a large PSU at the age of 20. As the first management trainee in the organization, I too had several ideas but soon realized that without mastering existing processes, meaningful change would not be possible. Young members of a family business must first understand the 'as-is' thoroughly before attempting to create the 'to-be' through digitalization and modern systems.

The PDP Group's efforts in building a strong organizational culture—such as its Employee Felicitation Program—have matured remarkably over the years. Its national recognition for Best Practices in Driver Management (2020) is another notable milestone. Celebrating

International Workers' Day as Drivers' Day within the organization reflects deep respect for the backbone of the logistics sector. This year-round commitment has resulted in an exceptional 95 per cent fleet utilization, despite the nationwide shortage of drivers.

In conclusion, I believe this book—whether one calls it a handbook or a guide—will be immensely valuable for young members entering their family businesses. It offers not just theory, but practical insights, lived experiences and actionable guidance.

I wish The PDP Group, Avishkar and all readers every success in their future journeys.

God bless.

—Sabyasachi Hajara
Former Chairman and Managing Director,
Shipping Corporation of India

Introduction

Statistics point out that around 85 per cent of Indian companies are family-owned businesses.[1] This type of business ownership forms the core of the Indian economy. It is also one of the oldest forms of business enterprise in the world. There is a misconception that family businesses are mostly seen in India and Asia. In fact, family businesses account for over 60 per cent of the GDP of the United States.[2] Similarly, over 60 per cent of companies registered in Europe are also family-owned enterprises.[3]

Therefore, the business that you may be inheriting, or have now decided to get involved in, is not something to be taken lightly. The opportunity to join the family business has enabled you to put your efforts into growing an existing

---

[1]Puri, Ronesh, 'The World of Family-Owned Businesses', *ET Edge Insights*, 10 February 2025, http://bit.ly/4gZJfkB. Accessed on 8 October 2025.

[2]Van Der Vliet, Daniel, 'Measuring the Financial Impact of Family Businesses on the US Economy', *FamilyBusiness.org*, 2 June 2021, https://bit.ly/46XGmMq. Accessed on 8 October 2025.

[3]European Commission, 'Family Business', https://bit.ly/4mXL0Qx. Accessed on 8 October 2025.

venture rather than starting a new company or working in the corporate sector under an unknown boss. You can choose to make sincere efforts to transform the family business you have joined. But how do you do that? I hope that, with the lessons I have learnt over the past 10 years working in my family business, I will be able to share some insights on what you can do to maximize your own potential, as well as the potential of your business.

Before we begin, let us understand what a 'family business' is all about. Many of you who pick up this book for the first time may wonder, 'Of course I know what a family business is… It's a business owned and managed by my family for maybe one, two or perhaps even more than three generations.' While that is true, to understand how to transform the family business, we must first grasp a key aspect. A family business is a 'commercial organization' where key decisions are influenced by members who are related by blood. This unique business setup has its advantages and drawbacks, which we will navigate over the course of this book.

Your family business could be in the hospitality, manufacturing, logistics, wealth management, sustainability, agricultural, automobile, tech or any other sector. The core principles of the family business, however, remain the same across all industries, though the work culture is different from what we see in corporate organizations. This is why various books on management and advanced courses in B-schools do not quite encompass the intrinsic forces working behind a family business. There are policies that could be implemented but are not even brought to the table due to the fear of hurting the sentiments of a family member. While it is encouraging to read books on professionalism and how-to-guides on balancing work and personal life, how do you actually manage that in a family business when you have to go home and talk to the same people you were in a board meeting with a couple of hours ago?

Yes, things are complicated; and that is why not many family businesses survive beyond the second generation. Many youngsters who join the family business are left in a dilemma. After all, we have received quality education from good schools and universities, we have friends of similar social background and we have not felt the struggle for survival during our teenage years. Once we set foot in our family businesses, we realize that things are not as 'glamorous' as they appeared when we were younger.

Our parents and grandparents built the family business from scratch, putting their precious time into it. The things we take for granted were once unattainable luxuries for them when they were our age. Hence, they do expect us to appreciate the family business and the opportunities at our disposal. And we youngsters do appreciate it—at least most of us do. However, during the initial days, we may experience a shock to the system and ask ourselves whether it is indeed worth grinding in the family business when we could move overseas to a nice corporate job. We may also find it difficult to relate to our employees, whom we perceive to have low ambition based on feedback received from senior family members and the limited role of employees in decision making, which actually comes down to the family business setup. This is partly because we have been exposed to a high quality of life from a young age, and we now realize the hard work ahead of us to take things to the next level in our own family-business setup.

Family businesses, especially small- and medium-scale companies, operate with optimum efficiency. To bring the family business to a certain level in highly competitive markets, the senior family members have worked relentlessly, putting in long hours year after year. The business is their passion, and they genuinely enjoy it. As a young entrant, you may feel proud of the family business, but it is definitely not your passion—at least not on day one. However, it is important to remember that most family businesses that have scaled up and transformed themselves could do so because the next generation overcame these initial doubts and implemented systems that benefitted both the business and the family members.

As we delve into the different chapters, I want you to remember that this book is written by someone who stood in your shoes just a few years ago. Someone who enjoyed a fun childhood, studied at a reputed university and then joined a family business. Someone who saw many opportunities, but was also very confused at times.

In the opening three chapters (Chapters 1–3), I discuss the importance of breaking through the privileged mindset often associated with the next-generation family business owners. These chapters focus on encouraging professionalism at office, understanding the importance of workplace culture and becoming aware of the importance of a clear mission statement.

The next three chapters (Chapters 4–6) shed light on critical areas often brushed aside as mere vanity in family businesses but are, in fact, crucial to a company's growth. These chapters explore the key role of human resources, the importance of not taking business networking opportunities for granted and the need to cultivate an attitude of lifelong learning.

The core of the book (Chapters 7–9) emphasizes the role

of creating robust systems to ensure scalability. It highlights the importance of consistent actions and emotional regulation when dealing with other family members involved in the business.

These core learnings lay the groundwork for self-reflection in the later section of the book (Chapters 10–12) by empowering you to acknowledge that you have the power to make a difference. This section further elaborates on the benefits of scheduling business activities and learning to say 'no' to things that do not resonate with your belief system.

Finally, the concluding section (Chapters 13–16) introduces a new philosophy of 'give and receive' that will enable you, the reader, to attract abundance in your life and motivate you to strive for harmony in your relationships with family members.

This is a practical book, grounded in the real-world experiences of a youngster in the family business. I hope you are able to incorporate some of the key practices that have helped us transform our family business from having a turnover of around INR 40 crore five years ago to over INR 200 crore revenue at the time of writing this book.

1

Bring Professionalism to the Family Business

In office, refer to your father as 'sir' and your mother as 'ma'am'.

Family businesses are unique. It is rare to find a commercial organization where the top management completely trusts one another. There may be decisions that certain individuals may not like, but everyone agrees that the individual taking the decisions has the best interest of the family business in mind. This mindset develops over time because the reputation of the family business directly impacts the personal reputation of each individual in the top management. Here, reputation carries a deeply personal meaning. Therefore, every individual is committed to serving to the best of their abilities. They may not always believe that their employees are giving their best (which is not a helpful notion to hold, and we will talk about this later), but they firmly believe that their family members are putting in their best efforts, even if results are not as expected.

As the older generation works tirelessly to establish the organization, they notice that it is mainly the family members who stick with them for the long haul. Most employees leave once their working hours are over, and this is something which is not really appreciated in the traditional work environment. We will discuss about the whole management–employee dynamics of the family business in the later chapters. For now, I would like to draw your attention to an essential mindset shift in the family business context: in office, refer to your father as 'sir' and your mother as 'ma'am'.

A small aside, before we get into the details—for youngsters entering the family business in the West, I would replace the words 'sir' and 'ma'am' with the actual names of your parents who are in the family business, as that is how most employees refer to their bosses in Western culture. In India, the salutations of 'sir' and 'ma'am' are used in almost all businesses in the small and medium sector.

Merely modifying the salutations may not have much of an impact. However, it is the first step towards transforming your family business. The moment you switch the salutations of your parents at home and in the office, you begin to create a division of the personal and professional self. What starts as a basic change in salutation slowly develops into a mindset that will help you maintain professional boundaries.

If you are someone who has recently joined your workplace and you begin referring to the company's head as 'dad' or 'Papa', you are subconsciously creating an undeserved hierarchy among your employees. Despite not having any prior experience in the company, you have gained a special status from day one. While I am not telling you to hide your identity and pretend to be someone else,

I am suggesting that you avoid creating status roles based on your surname and instead focus on how you can add value through your work.

The moment you enter the boss' chamber and feel that the space does not belong to your dad but to the head of the company, your intrinsic behaviour will start changing. It may not be a big change on day one, but after a few weeks, you will start taking more accountability of things because you simply cannot get the work done by pleading the case to your 'dad' and convincing him. The moment you know that you must convince your 'boss' and not your father, you will have to dig deeper and explain your strategies and your reasonings. You will recognize that although you have the opportunity to present your arguments and persuade your boss, you do not have the personal space to throw tantrums at the workplace or plead with your father to accept your proposals irrespective of merit. The roles will get well-defined, and it will have a positive ripple effect on the senior members of the company as well.

If you are already working in a family business, or if you are planning to join your business soon, then you may be taken aback with this approach initially. It may even seem unnecessary, and your own parents might discourage you from doing this. It is true that you can maintain a professional boundary without using professional titles to address your parents. However, even if you are maintaining that boundary internally, it will not be visible to those around you. So, if you have a vision for transformational growth in your family business and wish to lead by example, then you must do things differently.

The first thing this approach does is that it infuses professionalism in the workplace. Other employees notice something different, something they may never have seen before, or even imagined before. Employees working in a traditional family business often feel that the rules are different for them and for the family members working in the organization. The moment you take the initiative of referring to the seniors in the family business in an official manner, they wonder why one of the family members is behaving this way.

Well, this is the first step to bridging the gap between 'us' and 'them'. Don't we all aspire to be Microsoft and Apple? We love watching their keynotes and the way the company culture sounds. We marvel at how relaxed their leaders are with their employees. And then we tell ourselves that we could never imagine our employees to have this mindset, and therefore it's just impossible to have this culture in our company.

But are you willing to take the first step towards building that workplace culture? Or will you simply resign to the belief that you are not going to reach that level anyway, so why bother? The choices are in front of us—either we take it upon ourselves and bring a change in our family business, or we continue the tradition and carry the resentment of watching things remain the same.

Personally, when I joined my family business, I took it upon myself to draw a clear line between the roles of a parent and a boss. Initially, there were times when I overstepped boundaries due to the status I had from day one as a family member. However, over time, and by following a disciplined approach of never referring to my parents as 'mom' and 'dad' in office, I gradually managed to split the roles. This also led to a healthy environment at home. You realize that you did not just spend two hours with your dad at office.

In fact, you spent those hours with your boss, and now the roles are changed at home.

I have heard so many youngsters mention how family businesses blur the lines between personal and professional lives, but I have never felt this at home. A huge chunk of the credit goes to the fact that I refer to my parents with professional salutations in the office.

This was a conscious choice when I joined, because I realized I would be spending most of my waking hours with my parents. In Indian families, it's common for members to live together or remain closely connected, and the thought of being together with your parents both at home and at work can feel daunting. During the early days, I would often chat with my parents at office, discussing personal matters such as events from a recent family function. One conversation would lead to another, and after leaving their chamber, I would feel a sense of disconnect with the work environment.

Upon reviewing the management books I had at my disposal, I started feeling a contradiction when it came to my values and my actions. I read various articles, but I soon discovered there are not that many tools to rely upon for a youngster joining an Indian family business. So I began taking my own initiatives, the first being a rule of addressing my parents with professional courtesy titles. Did it feel strange initially? Perhaps. But did both our professional and personal relationships improve after this? Absolutely!

To my reader: I would like you to take out some time and reflect on whether your professional and personal relations with your family members tend to blur. You will probably realize that switching roles during professional and personal interactions becomes a challenge. This is a major concern for most newcomers entering the family business, and that's why differentiating the way you refer to your relatives at home and at work can have a sustained positive impact in maintaining good relations.

It may appear daunting at first to switch from referring to your relatives as 'papa', 'uncle' or 'ma' to using more formal forms of address in the workplace. I would recommend that you have a chat with your relatives regarding this and explain why this change would have a positive impact in your family life and your professional growth. After all, communication is the key to relationship building. This approach will ultimately impact your organization's culture in a positive manner, something I will discuss further in the next chapter.

2

Your Office Culture Is Your USP

Be ruthless in setting your organization's culture.

Organizational culture? What does this even mean? Perhaps it's something reserved for those big multinationals or those publicly listed corporations? No! That's not true. Your organization has its own unique culture, and it already exists. You don't know what it is? Well, it may be because it has never been clearly identified or articulated in words.

Perhaps the seniors in the company have been so focused on growth and operations that they haven't had the time to think about this aspect. This is completely understandable. But that's where you come in. You are the one who has the opportunity and the responsibility in shaping your organization's culture.

Sounds exciting!? It is. But it also comes with its own set of challenges, and the journey will truly test your character.

Today, my organization is certified as a 'Great Place to Work', by Great Place to Work®, India, for five consecutive years.[1] We were also conferred with a national award by the Confederation of Indian Industries for 'Best Practices in Employee Value Proposition'. I share these achievements with you because what seems so wonderful now felt impossible a decade earlier.

Just like most Indian family businesses, ours has a central figure—my father. He is a dynamic individual with a keen interest in making the workplace thrive. In many ways, I was lucky, for he always enjoyed listening to new ideas and meeting with youngsters. Later in my career, I realized that this was not a common trait. That said, while his vision strongly focused on employee welfare, the results were not being fully felt across the organization. This was a point of concern for him too.

Often, we resign ourselves to the belief that we are doing our best, but it's just 'bad luck' that people fail to recognize the efforts that the management is putting in. A careful and objective analysis of facts, however, helps us realize that very few things actually happen due to bad luck. However, to undertake such an analysis we must give time and effort. And the older generation unfortunately could not afford to do this because they were busy setting up the business.

Youngsters, on the other hand, have a unique opportunity for a value proposition here because they are not joining the business when it is at a survival stage. The business is usually at a level where the individual has the privilege to take some time out and invest their early years in understanding

---

[1]'Certified Companies List', *Great Place to Work,* https://tinyurl.com/5554arxs. Accessed on 13 October 2025.

how to shape the organization's culture.

It is important to begin this task early because shaping an organization's culture is a time-consuming process. Cultures are not created overnight. They take time to blossom, and they require tinkering and modifications along the way. The vision must be clearly defined, and plans should be laid out to achieve it. Obstacles on the way must be dealt with in a professional manner, and the culture should never be created by force. No culture can—or should—survive by force. It can only thrive if the people contributing to it firmly believe in the vision.

This vision, in turn, should be employee-friendly, ambitious, knowledge-driven and growth oriented. It is very difficult to define such a vision, and even more difficult is to lay a pathway to achieve it. That's why your first step should be to spend time talking to people in your company.

You should assume that much of what employees tell you about the company is because of your status as the next-generation member of the family business. You should not get carried away hearing rosy praises of how wonderful the company is. Instead, begin with the most effective word in the English dictionary—'why'. Any time you hear a person mention that they like something about the company, ask them, 'Why?'

Asking the right questions and actively listening to the responses will help you gain immense insight into the thought process of your people. I have realized that most problems and most inter-personal disputes start at a very minor level, and all it needed was for someone to step up and ask the question, 'Why did this happen?', instead of saying, 'These things happen. Ignore it and move on.'

Yes, the resolve to keep the operational engine running

is paramount in any business, but the need to ask why a problem happened is equally important. We often end up resolving the symptoms of a sickness instead of focusing on finding the root cause of the disease. This is why it is essential to engage with employees across all levels and seek their insights—to understand what needs fixing before embarking on the journey of creating a sustainable workplace culture.

Once an honest employee feedback process has been carried out, youngsters working in the family business must come up with an organizational plan. This plan must ensure that a new system emerges, where:

- individual responsibility is clearly assigned;
- a reward system that is data driven is put in place;
- confidentiality is maintained when someone reports behavioural issues;
- recruitment is based on sincere interviews instead of simple referrals of family members or managers; and,
- senior persons, including managers, are held accountable for lapses in discipline.

Now, several factors must be considered and acknowledged when setting out such a framework for workplace culture. Let us approach it with the acronym, SMART. This means that the framework must be:

- **S**pecific
- **M**easurable
- **A**chievable
- **R**ealistic
- **T**imely

First, the framework needs to be *specific*. You cannot devise a framework with a mindset that behavioural issues will be dealt in this particular manner, but if person 'X' is involved, then the rules will be modified in other ways. Such frameworks are destined to fail. Rules must apply equally to everyone. And while slight variations may be allowed keeping practicality in mind, the essence of the workplace culture will never come to fruition if we make modifications for every new case. You must remember to stay within the framework—and make exceptions only when there is a real good reason.

Second, the framework must have ways by which you can *measure* its effectiveness. There should be clear benchmarks to assess how much of the framework is being followed after a few weeks, a few months or a few years. You must have points of references in place to understand whether you are moving towards the goal, standing still, or drifting away from your vision. If the framework is not measurable, you may continue working without understanding whether you are making any progress. This would lead to a loss of enthusiasm, demotivating you from striving towards a transformative workplace culture.

Third, the framework must be *achievable*. Transforming workplace culture is a gradual process—it requires baby steps before the organization can eventually soar and perhaps become a leading multinational firm. However, you can't lose sight of the starting place. Simply put, a framework must not involve jumping from Step 1 to Step 10! In family businesses, employees are often accustomed to a certain pattern of working, and drastically changing the pattern will create uncertainty and resistance. It is, therefore, important to take the entire workforce along and create a framework that seems achievable. Yes, the framework can become more refined in due time, but it should not begin as a steep mountain that no one wants to climb.

Fourth, the framework must be *realistic.* We have to consider the resources at our disposal and plan accordingly. As youngsters entering the family business, we often have broader exposure than most of our employees and even some senior family members. Therefore, it is easy to get carried away by fanciful notions that may sound good in writing but are almost too unrealistic to execute. There must be a well-defined investment plan laid out in your framework, providing a tangible reference point for execution.

Fifth, the framework must be *timely.* You cannot create a plan for cultural transformation and set the timeline to achieve it as 20 years. We have all done various school projects, and what is the one thing in common for us all? If the deadline was 30 days away, most of us started working on day 28 or 29! Therefore, to maintain momentum, your framework must include well-defined timelines, checkpoints and periodic reviews. This will help both you and your employees to stay motivated during the process.

Once the framework for transforming the workplace culture is in place, the real work begins—putting the process in motion. This is when obstacles may come along the way.

In family businesses, we often have people who have become quite comfortable with their way of working. Some senior managers may have long-standing relationship with your elder family members and feel that they now have a secure future. There is nothing wrong in this, especially in a country like India where job security often takes precedence over most other professional aspirations.

The issue with job security, however, is that it does not

like the unknown. And it is in the unknown that change, and growth, occur. In a traditional work environment, an employee who seeks security would not want to change something that was working well for them. This is where you will need to have clearly defined policies with no exceptions.

If there is a rule about arriving to the office at a certain time, either make it flexible for everyone or not at all. The moment flexibility is granted for select few without transparent reasoning, you create an environment that is only going to deteriorate over time. This is where ruthlessness is required. If you want to transform your workplace culture and take things to the next level, well, be prepared to make a few people really unhappy. However, I assure you that if your intentions are honest and your impartiality consistent, you will win these people back in due time. These security-seeking individuals will either leave the organization because they don't want to change, or they will adapt, evolve and ultimately thank you for it!

Resistance may also come from within the family. There may be suggestions to focus on the financial side of the business instead of spending or rather 'wasting time' changing the workplace culture. It is natural to be attracted to things that give quick results and immediate gratification. Committing to a process that requires sustained effort, patience and discipline may not seem to be an attractive option. You may even question why you should waste time on your company's culture when you could be spending it thinking of a new project and increasing your turnover manifold.

Well, you certainly can—and I wish you the best of luck in your endeavours. But do remember that even those projects will take a few years of hard work. However, if you spend those same years focusing and transforming your workplace culture, it will help you build a competent team and a strong infrastructure. Focusing on your workplace culture now will help you take up multiple projects simultaneously in the future and have both motivated and talented individuals in your corner who will believe in your vision. They would be happy to work with you to bring all those projects to success.

Stay focused on the path to transform your workplace culture, and be unwavering and ruthless in your vision to create an environment you would feel proud to work in as an employee.

To my reader: What are some goals which you would like your family business to achieve? In which ways would investing time and energy to improve your organizational culture help you reach these goals? Once you have thought about this, have an open discussion with your family members about your objectives and the importance of setting the right organizational culture.

The views of senior family members may differ from yours, and it is important to have multiple rounds of discussions and reach a common ground. There could be some uncomfortable interactions along the way, but this is necessary to ensure everyone is aligned on the organization's collective goal. After all, a company's vision and mission are not just fancy words for the company website; they are, in fact, a blueprint that will guide your organization's journey like a compass that keeps it on course. I will elaborate on this in the next chapter.

3

Create Your Organization's Mission Statement

Set a clear company vision to inspire and transform your workplace.

As a teenager, there was one question our elders never failed to ask us, whether at family gatherings, weddings or casual visits. We too learned to ask it of our younger siblings and their friends. It was a question we heard so often that it almost became a ritual of growing up. What was that question?

> What's your ambition? What do you want to be when you grow up?

You are now a new entrant in your family business. You are carrying the hopes of your elders and your employees. You have a lot of plans and dreams. But are you clear on what your organization itself wants to be? As a young leader, wouldn't you want everyone associated with your company to understand the company's goals? Wouldn't you want them to know the destination you are leading them towards?

Wouldn't you want them to have a sense of how they are going to achieve these common objectives?

You would! And that's the reason you need to clearly lay out your organization's mission statement. Simply put, an organization's mission statement reflects upon your company's products or service offerings, the fundamental reason why your company exists and how your company plans to make an impact. It highlights the aims and the values of your company. Typically, a mission statement comprises a vision, a mission and your organization's key value drivers.

Here's a small activity. Sit with your elders and create your organization's vision. A vision must be something that is very ambitious, possibly the ultimate goal of your company. It should also showcase the process that your company will follow to achieve this ultimate goal.

Oh, and this must be defined in a single sentence!

Sounds tough, right? Well, it is! Crafting your company's vision is the foremost activity when it comes to creating a workplace culture. Every stakeholder of your organization deserves to know what your company's vision is.

There may be situations where your employees, vendors and clients are aware of your company's vision but they do not know how they can contribute to achieving it. We will address that later in this book. For now, the first goal is to create awareness. Until we are aware that our organization needs to have a vision, we can't truly begin the conversation about it.

Amazon's vision statement is:

> To be Earth's most customer-centric company, where customers can find and discover anything they might want to buy online.

They did not come up with this vision in a day. To summarize the ultimate goal of an organization in one sentence is indeed a task that will require a lot of analysis, internal discussions and passionate debates. The company's vision is what will define the organization culture, both consciously and sub-consciously.

My company's vision is:

> To become the benchmark company in the Indian logistics industry by building cross functional digital set-ups, upskilling workforce, developing infrastructure and leveraging resources of group companies.

Once the vision is defined and written down, the company's mission must be laid out, which usually refers to the core functions of the company that will help attain the vision.

My company's mission is:

> To provide efficient logistics support by seamlessly integrating our various service offerings and delivering professional services with a personal touch.

You must also analyse and lay down your key value drivers—the factors that make your organization unique. Regardless of the industry, competition is always present, and these key value drivers help you gain an edge over the competition. Every organization should have at least three identifiable key value drivers.

My company's key value drivers are:

- Experienced management team
- In-house integrated infrastructure

- Digitalized operational process
- Motivated team of employees
- Optimal use of resources
- Strong credit worthiness

Key value drivers do not need to be extraordinary. Take, for instance, having a 'motivated team of employees'. From the outside, this may seem quite basic—after all, many companies can have a motivated workforce. So, how is this a competitive advantage for me? Well, this is where implementation kicks in.

Simply writing down a detailed mission statement comprising the organization's vision, mission and key value drivers is not enough. These are just words written on a piece of paper. The next step is implementation. Once you have clearly laid out the mission statement, you need to strive towards strengthening your key value drivers.

For example, if an organization identifies 'in-house infrastructure' as a key value driver, then the leadership team must chalk out a plan on making systematic investments to strengthen their infrastructure. Similarly, if an organization places 'knowledge of subject matter' as a key value driver, then they must create a culture where upgradation of subject matter knowledge is a key factor when it comes to promotions, incentives and recognition.

The fact of the matter is that an organization's mission statement provides a guideline for where the organization wants to go. It is up to you, the next-generation leader, to build upon these value drivers and efficiently execute the mission, which will lead your company one step closer each day to attaining that ultimate goal.

In our company, we created our mission statement back in 2016. We uploaded it to our website and informed our employees. However, I made a mistake in how I communicated it. I assumed that by holding a few sessions on the importance of the company's mission statement and by pointing everyone to the relevant section on our website, my work was done. I felt confident that my employees now clearly knew our company's vision and mission.

Unfortunately, that was not the case. In fact, in 2023, we conducted an activity and found that even the top management couldn't recall a single key value driver of our company! This made me wonder where we had gone wrong. After all, I had discussed the mission statement with my seniors before setting it. We were all in agreement on the vision, mission and key value drivers. Then how is it that none of us could recall them?

The issue was a lack of repetition. I understood from this experience that the power of repetition is a leader's best friend. In fact, Jeff Weiner, former CEO of LinkedIn, explained this beautifully in an interview with *Business Insider.* Quoting a friend who in turn had paraphrased David Gergen, American political commentator and presidential adviser, Jeff said: 'If you want to get your point across, especially to a broader audience, you need to repeat yourself so often that you get sick of hearing your own voice—and only then will people begin to internalize what you're saying.'[2]

Taking this insight to heart, I changed our company's approach. We made sure to talk about the company's mission

---

[2]Blodget, Henry, 'LinkedIn's CEO Jeff Weiner Reveals the Importance of Body Language, Mistakes Made out of Fear, and One Time He Really Doubted Himself', *Business Insider*, 22 September 2014, https://tinyurl.com/2pzkttpc. Accessed on 13 October 2025.

statement at every possible occasion, whether it was an employee's birthday celebration, or ethnic day programme at the company, or even a weekly team meeting. After a few months we noticed the change. Employees actually started discussing about our vision and mission. Some even gave us feedback on what we could add as a key value driver.

The key learning from this exercise was simple: once we have invested the time to create a company's mission statement that we are satisfied with, we must ensure that the message is communicated on a regular basis to the entire workforce. Just as we work on our operations daily and become better at our vocation because we practise it each day, we must also become better at explaining the ethos of our company.

It took us around six to seven years to realize that communicating the company's mission statement is as important as training the workforce on technical aspects of their job. Now that we have made this activity an ongoing practice, we are noticing the change. Employees now feel a greater sense of purpose and understand how they are not just a cog in the wheel but active contributors to the company's vision. This exercise of communicating the company's mission statement has no end date—it is a continuous process, just like how there is no end to gaining knowledge of subject matters.

To my reader: Where would you like to see your family business in the next five years? Do you want it to continue gaining more market share in the current sector? Would you consider diversifying into new product or service lines? Do you see your family business expanding to different regions in the country or perhaps in a new international location? Perhaps, reflecting on these questions will help you realize what you want for your organization. This activity, along with discussions with your family members, will help pave the groundwork for setting your company's mission statement.

Creating a company's mission statement takes time, effort and patience. Unfortunately, you do not have infinite time, and it is not possible to do everything on your own—conducting market research on the industry, upskilling your own knowledge base, communicating workplace culture to everyone, following up on the mission statement, and so on. To grow, create and sustain a strong workplace culture, you must utilize the human resources (HR) department. I will discuss this in greater detail in the next chapter.

4

Invest in a Human Resource Department

Your organization's employees are your biggest brand ambassadors.

Human resources? As a family-owned business, do I really need to spend money on an HR department whose only role is to mark employees late and manage payroll? HR departments are for those fancy corporates, right? Surely, they have no place in a small family run organization where owners are involved in day-to-day operations…

Yes, the above feeling is completely understandable, and I suggest you review your thoughts with an open mind. Although our country is making great strides in digitalization and infrastructure development, India has not yet been able to fully utilize its human resources. As a youngster growing in a family business, you may have heard from your parents or relatives how there is a difference between a family member and an employee. You may have also heard how employees will never understand the pressures of a family business, and therefore cannot really be trusted with big decisions.

I don't blame our elders for thinking this way. They grew up in a different environment, and they spent so much of their hard-earned time building this platform for us. They did not have time to understand the subtle nuances of managing human resources because, to be frank, they had more urgent things to do like establishing a business in the first place and then ensuring its survival. However, you are joining the business with a new mindset and a different set of goals. You have the responsibility to take things to the next level. Therefore, setting a human resource or HR department is important for you.

When was the last time you conducted a professional interview in your family business? Chances are that you got a reference of an aspiring candidate and hired that person based on word of mouth, with a hope that the individual would perform their duties to the company's satisfaction. A slightly more organized family business would have an interaction with the aspiring candidate before offering the job. An even more systematic family business would put a job offer online, and the senior manager would conduct the interview to understand the employee's prior work experience.

Unfortunately, this hiring process will not take your company to the next level because it is based on 'reference' and 'hope'. Hiring people based on reference and hope is never a good plan, as every new hire shapes the office dynamics without you realizing it. When performance drops, it's easy to blame employees. But what if I told you that the employees may not be at fault for poor performance? More often than not, it is the management that is responsible. While it may sound harsh, this is usually what I have observed in most family businesses. We neglect the hiring process and the human resource element of our business.

By investing in an HR department, what I mean is to hire qualified professionals who are well-versed in recruiting, training, developing and engaging your workforce. You have to move past that mental block where human resource is limited to attendance and payroll management. You must understand that a qualified HR team is not a luxury anymore, but a requirement. You need an independent department to monitor your team of ground staff, associates and managers.

The reason many employees are not able to perform to their fullest potential is generally not due to a lack of talent. It is due to a lack of belongingness, or issues with their immediate reporting manager. You will never have the time or the ability to handle these issues. You have to accept the fact that most of your employees will sugar-coat the negative aspects of the company when speaking with you because you are the owner. You will therefore need to have qualified professionals who are confident to speak with employees, and to work with them during times of stress.

You will need to invest in a department that will provide unbiased and unfiltered feedback to you, without trying to please your ego. A department like that will start changing the fortunes of your organization. Your employees will feel trusted, and they will finally have that necessary bridge between them and the management.

The HR department doesn't exist to motivate employees, or give them a pep talk. They are present in an organization to show the management the mirror. They will let you know what your employees actually think about your company. If you are ruthless in your vision to create a transformative workplace culture, then you must be focused on hiring an independent set of individuals who will help you in this process.

I will share an experience from our own family business. For a long time, we too were unfamiliar with the need for a robust HR team. It was my sister, a counselling psychologist, who first introduced us to the concept of 'industrial/organizational psychology'. Initially, I dismissed it as another fancy term that may not work in the Indian context. However, we ended up giving this a shot and hired our first industrial psychologist in 2015.

Employees, especially the senior managers, were completely confused with this new hiring. They wondered why the company had hired a 'psychologist', and some even joked that strange experiments were to be conducted on them!

But as the industrial psychologist started working and conducting training sessions, we gradually uncovered trends in our organization that we were unaware of. We found out that the reason one of the employees in our documentation team was inefficient was not because they lacked focus or that they were not committed. It was simply because their reporting manager was dismissive of them, taunting them daily about how they expected yet another mistake. This constant criticism had had such a huge impact on the employee's confidence, and we would never have understood it without seeking professional assistance.

I had spoken with this employee personally many times, but they never once mentioned the issue. In fact, they always said that they would try to pay more attention in the future to minimize the constant errors they were making. Our management reviewed the case upon receiving the inputs from the industrial psychologist, and we took action. Today, the same employee is heading our documentation team. The employee's work environment became significantly more positive after we took steps against the senior who was perhaps great at their work but not at dealing with people.

This is one of several small incidents that we uncovered and resolved over time, thanks to the presence of an HR department with independent charge. Hiring qualified professionals in the HR department has enabled us to build teams with minimal bias and a workplace culture where employees are certain that even if all their issues can't be resolved, at least their concerns will be heard. They have faith that the management would try their level best to fulfil their requests.

Our hiring process includes a telephonic round of interview, filling up a customized CV template with professional questions, and a physical or virtual interview with the HR team and the reporting manager. Candidates who clear these rounds undergo a psychometric assessment to understand their suitability in the workplace and the type of persons they would get along with.

All this may sound really fancy, and you may feel that you don't really 'need' to do this. It's true! You don't really need to do a lot of things, but if you have a vision to transform your family business, then you need to start doing things that very few companies are doing. The benefits will far outweigh the costs. You will end up creating a workplace that is trusted by your employees, and improved employee productivity will have a domino effect on your organization's productivity. There is a unique satisfaction in seeing your systems and processes positively impact the people who drive your business forward.

In most family business, key decisions are made by family members. This gives a great incentive for the senior managers to be close to the family. There is nothing wrong in this, of course. They are doing the smart thing, and anyone in their position would do the same. Problems arise when they put all their effort in executing management's directions, instead of understanding the grievances of their subordinates, which directly or indirectly hampers the company's productivity. The senior managers continue showcasing to the family members how they are managing all works efficiently without passing much credit to the other team members. Meanwhile, junior employees, who do not have direct access to the management, hesitate to voice their opinions for the fear of repercussion.

By introducing an external stimulus in the mix in the form of an independent HR department, you change the rules of the game. By changing the rules of the game, you influence a change in the workplace culture. Managers may no longer be at ease knowing that an independent audit is carried out internally to understand workplace satisfaction, and to understand why certain employees in a particular department are not performing to their fullest potential.

Yes, this may lead to a temporary loss in productivity, as the attention of the senior managers may shift from focusing on operations to handling the current crisis of changed dynamics. But rest assured, if you have hired an honest group of HR professionals and have granted them genuine independence, there will be no long-term harm to the organization's productivity. On the contrary, the productivity of your family business will grow manifold when employees start considering themselves as 'team members' whose roles play a key part in attaining the company's vision.

With a structured HR department, you will also gain insights on the changes that employees at the ground level are appreciating. I believe this to be the most important aspect of transforming your family business. We are so focused on top-down approaches that we fail to even realize the opportunities at our disposal to maximise the potential of employees at the ground level. Relying solely on feedback from our immediate senior managers means we end up interacting with the employees at the ground level only once or twice a year. This is understandable, because we don't really have the time to speak to each and every person, and moreover we are not sure how the person at the ground level will react if we start taking updates from them on a regular basis. It may cause a sudden change in workplace dynamics which we do not want.

This is another reason why a structured HR department is needed in any business. It acts as a bridge between leadership and staff, giving sufficient time and attention to all sections of your workforce. Such a department eventually fosters a holistic and participative work environment.

When you were studying in your college, whether in India or abroad, you must have had a dream to implement several new initiatives in your business. However, you did not know where to begin. Moreover, you were probably showered with comfort from the very first day when you joined the family business. Perhaps your parents were relieved that finally their child was joining the company to help them! Perhaps your employees had a sense of security knowing that the business was going to flourish as the new generation was showing interest in it.

All of this is heartening, but you need to remember what you felt about your business when you were on the outside looking in. Were you satisfied with the way things were being run, or did you feel that you could make things better with new ideas? Did you wonder why corporate organizations have a better working structure and why your company lacks professionalism? Did you ever think your family business looked less dynamic or 'unglamorous' by comparison, and wondered whether you could work in such an environment?

Ask yourself these questions, and you will realize that our family businesses require constant upgradation. Every senior person is focused on increasing the company's turnover, and rightly so. The question here is whether you want to shoulder the same responsibility, or whether you want to build a strong foundation now by investing in your company culture. Doing so will not just quadruple your company's turnover in the coming years but also ensure sustained growth with a trusted, high-performing team. In order to achieve this vision, you must start investing in professionals who will take care of recruiting, training and implementing employee-welfare programmes.

To my reader: Make a list of tasks that distract you from focusing on your core goal of growing your business. Do you find yourself spending a large chunk of your day firefighting just to keep things running? If you could invest in human resources and delegate such tasks, how would you spend this additional time to grow your business? An honest introspection will help you realize the far-reaching benefits of investing in an HR department.

Once you have clarity, discuss your thoughts with your senior family members. It is essential to take initiatives and create the conditions for a positive work environment where key decision-makers have time to focus on bigger goals rather than daily operational hurdles. With basic systems in place and a motivated workforce, you will finally have the time to focus on growing your business through the art of public dealing and networking, something I will talk about more in the next chapter.

5

Earn the Opportunities for Public Dealing

Assess what value you add as a business owner during networking and client meetings.

As a youngster joining the family business or having been part of it for a few years, you will soon realize that there are lot of opportunities for public dealing at your disposal. You have access to the family's established network and resources, and you can start accompanying senior family members to visit key clients. During these moments, always ask yourself, 'What do I bring to the table?'

Let's be honest—at the beginning, you are only getting these opportunities because of your status as the next generation in the family business. It is therefore easy to approach these meetings with a laid-back attitude and simply see how things go. In the early days, you may visit key clients without much preparation and feel happy to be introduced as the son, daughter or relative of the senior family member. If this is happening, pause and take note. You have already entered into a safe zone in your mind due to the privilege of your family name.

Over time, this comfort may lead to a casual approach, and an over-reliance on the advice of the senior family members. You may find yourself in a situation where you constantly seek instructions from senior family members on how to deal with customers. In doing so, you fall into a pattern where your own contribution becomes passive.

This happens because, early in your career, your mind is a blank canvas. You absorb what you see and latch on it. You start thinking that your family's approach to client interactions is the ultimate method because:

- you assume that the current way of customer dealing is the best;
- you find comfort in the safe zone, as you are meeting customers with a senior family member who has already built a good rapport;
- you begin to take long-term customers for granted by assuming they will continue their association with your company simply because the senior family members have a good rapport with them; and
- you gain a false belief that you are adding value to the client dealings by simply being present.

The issue here is that you have started such an important part of the business—public dealing—from an already secure position. Our parents and grandparents did not have that privilege. Despite not having the best formal education, they understood how tough it was to even get one meeting with a particular client, which perhaps took over six months of relentless follow-ups in some cases. They knew they had a very short window of opportunity to convince the customer, and it was up to them to make the most out of it.

You, on the other hand, may not have had to work as hard to schedule an appointment with that customer. You were simply lucky that you were handed an opportunity to meet such an important customer by virtue of your family position. You therefore do not realize what a big opportunity you have got, and hence you do not really prepare for the moment. You go with the flow.

Becoming aware of this phenomenon is essential. I always found myself feeling aimless during my initial client interactions. I was being treated well, yet everything just seemed 'okay'. There was no thrill. Perhaps a certain degree of challenge is needed to make actions enjoyable. I realized that if I did not have the tag of being a family member, I would not be invited to these meetings so early on in my career. Therefore, I had to embark on a journey of self-assessment to understand whether I was truly ready to attend these meetings. I had to ask myself, 'What do I bring to the table?'

This attitude helped me in my self-development path, and it enabled me to gain a sense of professionalism. I started to understand that I have the privilege to attend any meeting which I want to, and so I must prepare myself to utilize this privilege for the company's growth. Despite having the opportunities to be present in any client meetings which were scheduled, I had to self-regulate my behaviour to 'earn' those opportunities. I had to spend more time with my reading materials and understand how to leverage a better position for my company during these meetings.

This mindset encouraged me to have detailed discussions with senior managers who regularly visited clients. More often than not, when I asked them the reason for visiting certain clients, their response would be that they had been instructed to do so. When asked about the agenda for the meeting, they would confidently say that they had discussed it with senior family members, and that they had been instructed on the areas to discuss.

I realized that there was a lack of personal agency when it came to meetings. Over time, we had slipped into a comfort zone where people had stopped thinking, finding peace in following instructions. This complacency threatened both personal growth as well as the growth of the family business. Ideas were originating from a single source; and no matter how brilliant that source, ideas need to be compared and analysed. More importantly, sharing of different ideas leads to constructive discussions and greater involvement of the workforce.

Starting this shift is not easy. It takes time to unlearn philosophies that have been followed for long periods and have been successful in the past. Yes, these philosophies have worked in the past and have helped your family business reach a certain level. However, transformation will not happen by following the same same things that got you so far. The thought process needs to be revisited and refined from time to time in order to achieve transformative growth.

If you have set a target for yourself to create a professional workplace, then you are beginning to understand the importance of compartmentalizing the personal and professional relationships with your family members. You have a clear understanding of your company's vision, and you are working towards creating a good working environment where your employees feel heard. You recognize the privilege you have received when it comes to visiting key clients, and this awareness drives you to conduct thorough preparation by analysing relevant data. You also try to acquaint yourself with past issues faced by your clients, along with feedback across all employee levels. This approach helps you get better prepared when figuring out what unique value propositions you could offer for establishing a more sustained relationship.

Once you realize how valuable it is to be well prepared when accompanying senior management during visits to key clients, you will encourage your managers to adopt the same mindset. Then, you will notice a change in the company culture. You will notice a reduction in the things that were being taken for granted. You will also understand that many managers who were simply following instructions in the past and were receiving a good growth trajectory due to this attitude are now finding it very difficult to independently think of strategies. While not every employee needs to develop strategic thinking skills, it is essential that senior non-family managers exercise personal agency. You have to inculcate a feeling where no-questions-asked obedience is not encouraged, but rather your employees realize the value of personal contributions in ensuring successful client visits.

The process of transforming your family business culture—from one where employees are happy simply following instructions to a new professional mindset where senior team members realize the importance of introspection and personal agency—is not going to happen overnight. In fact, you will be deeply mistaken to believe that you can achieve this by yourself.

As youngsters, we often feel that we can get our desired results by putting our foot down and pushing through anything that comes in the way. Such methods often lead to a lot of collateral damage and employee grievances because the rationale for change is not properly communicated.

In fact, even some of your own family members may question the need to bring a mindset shift amongst employees. After all, their perspectives have been shaped over decades of growing the business in an era without technology or real-time data. Senior family members have consistently rewarded employees for their ability to follow instructions and get work done without asking too many questions. During those times, this working style was perhaps considered to be in the best interests of the company.

It is therefore crucial to first communicate to your senior family members the benefits of transforming the work environment. Employees must be seen as more than hired hands for getting tasks done. You must share with the senior members how employees can become accountable and proactive when given the freedom to exercise personal agency in their work.

Times are changing and the methods that worked back in the day may no longer be appropriate for taking your business to the next level. In today's work environment, where data is abundant and AI tools such as Perplexity, ChatGPT and Gemini are widely accessible, disruptions are occurring faster than ever. Training senior employees to develop an adaptive mindset will lead to greater accountability and, in turn, drive company growth. After all, the success of the family business is everyone's ultimate goal.

Speaking of the agency of employees, here is an interesting thought to dwell upon: why is it that in the Indian family business structure, we hardly see employees attending trade meets and seminars? It is mostly family members who attend these seminars, and that is because there is an inherent understanding that only the owners can make important decisions.

While we are seeing a slight growth in the presence of employees in these seminars, there is still a long way to go for small- and medium-sized companies. We are fixated on the idea of projecting the business owner as a larger-than-life figure. Yet, the true role of the business owner is to make smart investments, oversee organization's policies and ensure that the business remains profitable while using its resources optimally.

In spite of this, many owners place unnecessary pressure on themselves and their family members by assuming responsibilities that can and should be delegated. This often stems from a deep-seated belief that the business can only function effectively if every crucial task is handled by a family member. A few examples of such belief systems are:

- The owner must personally recruit every single candidate because employees cannot be trusted to hire.
- The owner must visit all the clients because the clients will not engage with employees.
- The owner must attend all training programmes to hone their skills because employees may take the training and leave.
- The owner must attend seminars as only then would the company gain new customers.
- The owner can delegate basic tasks to employees, but every important decision must be taken by them.

The above thought process limits your growth opportunities. Instead, giving the right opportunities and upskilling your workforce will bring long-term sustained benefits to your organization. It is not possible for you to spend time networking and growing your business if you are busy micromanaging your organization's activities. Public dealing is an art, and I have learnt from experience that the best networkers are those who have a strong system in place that enables them to give their undivided attention to potential clients.

In 2022, I joined Business Network International (BNI), the world's largest business networking and business referral organization. Over the years, I have interacted with hundreds of business owners and realized that it is important to listen attentively to the other person. This is only possible once you have a team of motivated individuals who carry out the company's vision while you effectively network to grow the business.

'Earning your opportunities for public dealing', the chapter title, means that you are not networking with an expectation to gain new clients simply because you own a family business. It means to invest time cultivating relations and taking ownership. Once you shape your mindset and approach public dealing with an honest intention of adding value to the other person's business, you automatically start building your own unique identity. You stop going with the flow, instead reflecting on how you are utilizing your time. You understand that you need to 'up your game' before entering the world of public dealing. You take personal responsibility of not being known just as your father's daughter or mother's son, and instead being recognized for what you are bringing to the table.

It could also lead to a different trajectory for the business. What if you perhaps realize that public dealing is not your forte, and you are more inclined to devise strategies? What if you realize that apart from your senior family members, no one is really capable of handling that one tough client? What if you understand that the client visits are mainly happening in an unplanned manner just to resolve issues, but there is not much focus on building a relationship?

There are a lot of 'what ifs' that come to the forefront once you start asking questions. While I would not ask you to keep dwelling on the 'what ifs' indefinitely, it is indeed important to focus on areas you have never considered before. Doing so will also help you build a roadmap on how the company's brand should be. We often ignore these aspects and leave brand building to those big corporates, as we feel our company does not need this at the current stage of growth. This is a self-defeating attitude. You are already resigned to the fact that you cannot really build your company's brand, or that you will build the brand once you reach a certain level. This is a vicious circle, waiting endlessly for the 'right time' to begin.

Asking questions and engaging in honest self-reflections will shape the way you perceive your family business. You will no longer be someone who simply goes with the flow and enjoys the inherited privileges. You will cultivate discipline in your thinking, and you will start behaving like a professional corporate leader who must put strategies in place. You will look inwards and analyse your family business as a company and not as your personal inheritance. This mindset will help you break the shackles of complacency, replacing comfort with a productive sense of discomfort—and eventually, a renewed enthusiasm for the new opportunities within your reach.

So yes, attend seminars, client meetings, training programmes and all those talked about public events. You will always have these opportunities at your fingertips, and no one will stop you from doing what you wish. But remember, you have to *earn* those opportunities! You must become self-disciplined and understand what you bring to the table. And if that answer does not come immediately, take time to introspect and dig deeper.

You are here to transform the family business, not to settle into a comfortable lifestyle and oversee the basic functioning of your company. Utilize the platform you have received by first becoming aware of the platform itself. Then, identify your strengths and focus on the things you need to work on. Dream big! Dream of building a workplace where you can train your employees to *think* and come up with strategies as well. Involve them in public dealings. You will receive great joy in seeing other people reach their full potential, and their development would lead to the growth of your family business. It would enhance employee satisfaction, and it would bring a sense of professionalism at work.

And what if some employees leave? Well, that is how things were meant to be anyway. You would rather have three smart managers in your firm than 10 managers who are only good at carrying out instructions.

If any opportunity comes your way, reflect on whether it has arrived purely because of your position in the family business. I would never suggest that you say no to any opportunities. You should, or rather you must use your privileges. Be grateful for it, but do not just drift along, following the easy path. Focus on how you can make the most of each opportunity and then proceed. Make full use of your position but do not take undue advantage of it.

You are in this business to change lives, and your image in the public should be of someone who has brought their own ideas in the business instead of simply carrying on the work of your predecessors. The results of your efforts will come in due time, and with them will arrive a sense of personal satisfaction that is truly priceless. Earning your public dealing opportunities will help you grow as an individual and strengthen those areas of your life that would have been completely ignored had you chosen to stay in that 'safe zone'!

To my reader: Have you ever felt that you would approach networking events and client meeting with more preparation if you were working as a senior manager in a corporate house instead of your own family business? Take out some time and analyse the meetings held by your company with key clients during the past three months. Check whether any of the meeting notes were documented or if there were internal meetings done to follow up on the client visits. If not, that's a great place to start. I would also encourage you to join associations which have networking at their core. This would enable you to meet like-minded people of different industries and observe how they conduct their businesses. Meeting new people with an open mind will help you create a culture of learning in your workplace. I will elaborate on this in the next chapter.

6

Think of Your Family Business as a Learning Organization

Take time to get an all-round perspective of your processes.

Learning is an essential part of our lives. It begins with the understanding that we don't know everything. We seek guidance from various sources, whether through books and videos or through the insights of intellectuals, family members, friends and peers. These teachings help us gain a deeper understanding of different concepts, and enable us to acknowledge the complexities present in our interconnected world.

In an organization, learning is usually imparted in a top-down manner. If the seniors of the company consider learning to be an important tool, that mentality flows down the line. As a youngster joining the family business or as someone working in the family business for a few years, there are certain factors related to learning that we must keep in mind.

Because you are a key person from day one, you will be surrounded by lots of comfort. Yes, there are expectations from senior family members when you join the business, but they are also quick to lay down the path in front of you. They tell you which areas to focus on initially and how to proceed once you gain experience. This is an important step, but it comes at a cost. As you attentively listen to the advice being given, your positive bias towards your family members usually hinders you from questioning whether the path laid out is appropriate for you. You begin to depend on their advice from the very first day, and it soon becomes a habit that is difficult to break later.

In such a scenario, it is important to train your mind to think of the family business as a 'learning organization' and yourself as a lifelong learner who introspects the logic behind your actions. In fact, the moment you begin to do so, your journey of self-reflection truly begins. You will no longer follow advice simply because of the status of the relative who is giving that advice to you, rather you will introspect whether the advice given is in sync with your mindset. If it is not, you will probe further and engage in dialogue with the family member to gain a better understanding of their thought process. These discussions with senior family members may not be easy to begin with, but the journey of transforming your family business was never going to be a bed of roses in the first place.

While engaging in dialogue with senior family members, remember that you are listening to understand their views and not reacting quickly just to prove a point. The purpose of dialogue is to convey that following an advice half-heartedly benefits neither you nor your business. Chances are that senior family members have the best intentions offering guidance, and those interactions may well point you in the right direction. However, there may be a slight chance that you would like to adapt their teachings in light of the knowledge and exposure you have gained through your education. I am confident that while senior family members want you to follow in their footsteps, they are equally interested in seeing you create your own identity. Cordial discussions and healthy debates will enhance your critical reasoning skills and bring greater clarity to your thoughts. By encouraging dialogue, you will help your seniors understand your personality better and in turn carve out your own unique identity in the organization.

The moment we start following a path without questioning it is the moment we stop learning in the true sense. In order to gravitate towards being a 'learning organization', we must be motivated to examine our existing processes and analyse the areas that need work. This may also require us to take a deep dive into areas that have been considered unimportant for a very long time.

I would like to give a simple example in this regard. As a person with a mindset to learn, I sat with one of our executives to understand how a particular document was being created. As the executive demonstrated how they first collected the data and then entered it into specific columns, I realized a few things. Initially, the executive was hesitant to speak to me but got much calmer over time. This was because I did not ask the executive any questions, rather I engrossed myself to understand their work. I was seeing that Excel sheet for the first time, and while this could be considered a very menial task for someone from the top management, I would like to emphasize that it was anything but menial. Observing it with fresh eyes gave me a new perspective on our workflow. Once the employee had carefully explained the entire process, I started working backwards to find how the data was received by the user, and how we could make that process faster. This led to interactions with other executives from different departments, and within a week, we discovered that this one basic Excel sheet required close coordination among four or five people.

In many family businesses, there are many similar background tasks that we see every day, but do not pay much attention to. We assume that such tasks are not meant for us, and that there isn't much value in getting to know more about a certain job. This is where we make mistakes because we assume things.

There have certainly been times when such exercises revealed no particular trend. However, even if you find one or two instances where you uncovered a trend and found out more about your business' working style based on the daily work of your people, you make a meaningful impact. Once your employees see that you are interested to learn how they perform their work and then you give your suggestions, you will often feel that the suggestions are well-received.

A learning organization is one where every single member is aware of their responsibilities and how their work impacts the company. This leads to the employees discussing new ways to enhance productivity, and they brainstorm steps to improve existing mechanisms with each other. An organization that is driven by the top management providing instructions and everyone else simply following it is a 'dormant organization'. This is because there is one-way communication, and feedback is neither appreciated nor taken seriously. It is an authoritarian mode of management where the business solely relies on the judgements of the people at the top.

At the inception of your family business, this approach was acceptable. Why? This approach made sense for several reasons:

- The older generation had to build the family business from scratch.
- They were often focused on making ends meet and surviving from one quarter to the next.
- The marketplace lacked a pool of skilled manpower, and most people joined businesses based on word of mouth or personal references.
- The family business had perhaps less than 10 employees.
- Digital technology was limited, and the market was niche, with little competition.

Times have changed. Competitors are upgrading themselves every single day. Start-ups are being established in the thousands. While the old ways may help you sustain your family business, you must focus on 'learning' to really transform the business to the next level. You have to work towards changing the status quo of your company from a 'dormant organization' to a 'learning organization' by enthusiastically encouraging two-way communication, which includes your conversations with your valuable employees.

The next time you review your balance sheet, operational process, client feedback, or any other business function where you are not sure what the data means, do not hesitate to ask questions. Questions could definitely be asked to your family members, but you shall also ask questions to your employees who are actively involved in the daily work.

If you find yourself thinking, 'What can my employees tell me? They'll just look at me in shock if I ask them for a question or suggestion,' then there is a lot of work to be done in building your company culture. In order to become a 'learning organization', you must empower your employees to develop the freedom to ask as well as answer questions and to apply their minds. Perhaps they have become so accustomed to taking instructions that they have blocked out that part of their mind that can think and question the instructions given to them. It could also be the case that they may not have the aptitude to think and are only capable of following instructions without taking individual responsibility. Either way, it is time to change.

I firmly believe that in order for an organization to achieve sustained growth, there must be a sincere intent to let go of employees who have failed to perform as per expectations or who may be good performers, but their attitude is detrimental to the overall workplace culture. This intent also creates opportunities for new entrants to work in your organization, and it makes senior employees realize that they cannot take their position in your family business for granted.

Now the important question here is who decides if an employee is or is not performing well, or whether the employee does or does not have the right attitude conducive to your workplace's culture. If these decisions of letting go of employees are based on personal feelings or opinions of senior family members, then I am afraid your family business will struggle to attract and retain top talent. There must be clearly-defined processes and responsibilities for every role, along with practical, data-driven evaluation mechanisms to assess performance objectively.

As a youngster in the family business, you may read this and think that the concept of layoffs is something reserved for large corporations. You may even feel uneasy thinking of letting go of an individual who may not be performing well but has a great equation with you and your family members. I know that this is not an easy topic to consider. And that's why it is crucial for the next generation of the family business to carefully understand this. There are reasons why so many family businesses have great potential, but they fail to reach the desired levels of success. In fact, it all leads back to my earlier chapters where I talk about bringing professionalism to the workplace. You must create structures and processes to ensure you are not evaluating individuals simply based on feelings and emotions, rather you are analysing their performance with data.

During my initial years in the family business, we had promoted an individual from our dock operations department based on his work performance and proactiveness in resolving critical shipment-related issues. The employee soon received the promotion letter. Confident that he would be motivated in his new role, I was surprised when he requested that we do not announce his promotion to his colleagues. When I asked him the reason for the same, he explained that his colleagues would no longer talk to him in a friendly manner if they found out he got promoted. This is because they would perceive him to be 'too close' to the management and fear that he would share all their conversations with them.

I was quite taken aback hearing this and then realized that as a family-run organization, we must learn that no matter how much structure we bring, the mindset and culture will not shift unless we communicate the evaluation process to each and every individual. If an employee got promoted, it could be interpreted as favouritism—that they were close to the family members; and if an employee received a warning letter or was being sacked, it could be perceived that they behaved badly or had a fallout with a senior family member or an employee close to the management.

We responded by initiating a transparent process: we not only announced the list of employees who got promoted but also gave clear data-based information on why they received the promotion. Did this activity change everyone's opinion overnight? No. But it was the right starting step. Over time, our employees have become comfortable sharing the news of their promotions with colleagues, as now the information flow is transparent and the criteria for promotion are clearly communicated.

For employees who are not performing well or have behavioural issues, the solution is not to remove them but in fact to have a sincere discussion with them. It is important to first make them aware of the areas they need to work on and give them time to improve. If things still do not change, the next step is to give a written letter reinforcing the areas where they require improvement along with a time frame for the next evaluation. It is only when this also does not lead to a positive change that you must evaluate whether it is worth having this employee in your business. While I fully acknowledge that letting go may be tough, but knowing that fair opportunity and clear guidance were provided allows you to move forward with closure. It also helps the employee learn and grow in their future professional journey.

The time taken to assign responsibilities to each individual is in itself a learning process for you and your entire HR department. At times, even line managers are not completely aware of the responsibilities of their subordinates. In the year 2016, we began the process of assigning roles and responsibilities to each of our 150 plus employees. We were taken by surprise when some line managers were asked to describe the responsibilities of their subordinates. They were blank when asked this question, or their answers were vague, such as: 'Person X performs all jobs well.' When probed further to specifically mention the daily activities, some could not muster up more than one point. This made us learn that there were some individuals who were not performing up to the mark, but it was not the fault of that individual. The person's line manager never gave them enough work, as there was not much incentive in developing the subordinate.

Once we informed these managers that we would give them some extra time, but we needed to know the roles and responsibilities of each of their subordinates, there was a change in the work atmosphere. Suddenly, people were panicking as they had been exposed to an unknown territory. They had to now sit and *think*! They had to come up with roles for their subordinates, something they never bothered doing before. It was a learning experience for them. Questions that were left completely for the family members were now in the domain of senior managers. These small steps help create a stronger, more professional culture over time.

You often wonder why your employees do not co-operate with each other or commit to your organization in the way you want them to. But unfortunately, you seldom take a step back to reflect that you are dealing with a different generation. You have grown up observing your parents and uncles work relentlessly to bring your family business to its current level. The older generation received immense support from employees who have stayed with the company for several years, sometimes even decades.

However, it is important to accept that times have changed, and the next generation of employees do not see themselves as working in a single company for life. Young professionals today want to work in a place where they feel valued and respected. The important thing to realize is that even if they really like the workplace, they may still want to switch to a different industry just to experience something new. When I speak with aspirational youngsters who have just passed out of college, I realize that most of them do not have the same dreams that the older generation had—a stable job, house ownership, a car or a desire to be perceived as a loyal employee. Many of today's youngsters are happy moving to different cities to experience life and explore their hobbies and interests instead of grinding long hours to climb up the corporate ladder.

For the older generation in the family business, it becomes tough to come to terms with this attitude because they often feel that youngsters ought to build their careers by working 12–14 hours a day because they had done the same many years ago. It is therefore really important for you, the next generation of the family business, to communicate and share your observations with your parents, uncles, or other senior members of the family business. Setting the right expectations is crucial to effectively communicate the need to transform your family business from a people-centric and silo-based setup into a system-driven and collaborative organization.

As you aim to scale your workplace, you must become more aware of the world around you. I am sure that at some point in the past year, you must have fallen into the distraction trap of those 30-second reels that promise to transform your workplace and boost team productivity. We feel inspired and try out the next fancy trend, only to lose steam after a couple of weeks when we don't get the intended results. It is important for you to see through the clutter and remember a simple fact: people like to repeat doing what they are appreciated for. Your workplace culture, therefore, will be shaped by the kind of behaviours and actions you choose to acknowledge and incentivize.

For most of our relatives, family business was all about survival, and it is through their sheer will that they have brought the business to its current level. Now, with the tools at your disposal, it is crucial to create a culture where learning and curiosity are appreciated, and petty politics are not rewarded. Do note that I am not asking to discourage, berate or punish employees who are involved in office politics or who are not being supportive to newcomers. Taking strict actions or reprimanding senior employees merely leads to resentment and loss of motivation.

A recent study by the *Asian Journal of Education and Social Studies* also highlighted that incentivizing positive behaviour is much more effective in achieving sustained change than punishing undesirable conduct.[3]

Unfortunately, in most family-run businesses, there is a lack of awareness on this topic. Thus, senior managers and employees do not feel incentivized to collaborate or work together. They remain busy protecting their job in the harsh business environment and ensuring that they do not do anything to offend the senior family members. This

---

[3]Dorji, Chheoku, 'The Power of Reinforcement Strategies: Evaluating Its Impact on Behavioral Change in a Bhutanese Classroom', *Asian Journal of Education and Social Studies,* Vol. 51, No. 6, 2025, 478–491, https://doi.org/10.9734/ajess/2025/v51i62011. Accessed on 16 October 2025.

attitude helps bring order; but too much order leads to creative blockage.

The fundamental requirement for a 'learning organization' is to have a culture where people have the freedom to question processes that, in their opinion, are not working well. They may be mistaken, and perhaps the process is actually perfectly fine. However, they need to have a platform to express their concerns, and you need the tact to explain the existing processes to them. What may seem like a waste of time in the initial stages, may lead to a 10× boost in productivity in a couple of years' time. Walking in your family business one day and seeing how employees are motivated to give their best without the fear of being shut down for their doubts is an exhilarating feeling. This is the next stage of transformation, where employees are no longer working as cogs in the system, but in fact they are playing a greater role in giving feedback.

A learning organization thrives on feedback from all sections of the workforce. And why just the workforce? Your organization also deals with various vendors who supply raw materials and inventories. Have you considered taking feedback from them, about how your employees interact with them? To grow and to transform, you need to be obsessed with receiving feedback and have the internal courage to listen to negative feedback as well. Criticism is inevitable when you are seeking opinions, and they must be taken in the right spirit.

Yes, at times you may feel that this exercise is completely pointless because you are spending time talking to people you pay (your vendors) just to have them critique your employees. Why would you do that? Well, do you know what the best judge of a person's character is? It's not how they talk to their seniors, but how they talk to people who are below them in the professional sphere. If you go to a hotel and you talk rudely to a waiter, it reflects a lot about you as a person. You would never talk to your boss or a senior family member in that way. So, by speaking with your vendors, you learn how your employees are behaving with them, and this helps you gain insight on the areas to focus on. Change takes place when parts of a machine are tinkered with. You will have to tweak the business environment if you want to instil a corporate culture.

When the culture of inquisitiveness and attentive listening flows from the top down, there is a change in the organizational environment. Folks are used to seeing instructions cascade from family members to managers, from managers to executives, and from the executives to lower levels. While you must run the business efficiently and I am not suggesting you to spend your entire working hours seeking opinions and approvals, it is important to encourage a culture of feedback. After all, the key question is: while keeping the company growing, how are you going to create a culture where your company is considered a 'learning organization'?

Continuous learning leads to sustained competitive advantage in the marketplace. So, isn't it better that instead of just the senior family members learning new tricks of the trade, the entire workforce joins hands in the process? Yes, the scale of the results will vary, but such a culture will be created that rewards constructive discussions, rather than a downward spiral of gossips and resentments. Resentment creeps in when people feel they are unable to live up to their full potential and that they don't have enough opportunities to express themselves at work. We all enjoy working at a place where we can provide inputs and feedback, instead of simply following instructions.

Imagine yourself at home. Your house is under renovation and your parents are deciding wall colours, the design of the floor tiles, the lights for the living room, etc. You wish to contribute, but unfortunately, you have never been asked about your opinions. It is reasonable to expect that you would still want to share your ideas, but sometimes you feel it's better to stay silent. You return to your room, and you resent the situation. You dislike the fact that your parents don't ask for your opinion, and you are further discouraged by your lack of courage to voice your views.

Now imagine, what if your parents came to your room and asked you about your views? You would probably be surprised and hesitate to respond at first. But what if they followed up and they were sincere in their efforts to get your feedback? You would then open up enthusiastically and share your design ideas.

Think of your office employees in the same way. Perhaps they do have ideas and suggestions, but they are just scared to voice their opinions. Perhaps they have never really done this before and now they believe it is too late. This is where you come in—the next generation! You can start taking those steps that others apparently don't have time for. You can ask for their views and appreciate them for voicing their opinions. It will lead to a constructive cycle of two-way feedback. Other people will also see that opinions are valued in this business, and they will have a renewed sense of purpose. Gradually, they will move beyond the routine and think of areas where they could suggest improvements. This will lead to a 'learning' attitude in your workforce, which will give long-lasting returns!

To my reader: Think of a project or a particular task that did not go as per expectations. Do you feel the results could have been different if you had genuinely invited inputs from employees other than your senior family members? After you have introspected on the above thought, I recommend you do a small activity for the next seven days. Prepare a list of some day-to-day activities of your organization, tasks which you feel are menial and are being performed as expected. Now spend some time interacting with the employees who are performing these tasks and take their suggestions on whether any minor improvements could be made. After seven days, think whether you learnt something after interacting with them. And over the next month, observe their behaviour to gauge how the employees must have felt to be asked about their views.

Small yet meaningful interactions will make huge long-term impact and help you realize the importance of treating learning as a continuous process. The goal of this chapter is to make you aware that behind every activity that you perform, there needs to be a sincere attempt to create a culture of 'learning'. There will always be resistance and negative reactions when something new is introduced. At times, you will also learn to course-correct based on the feedback received. By recognizing the importance of 'learning', you will not feel deterred; instead, you will experiment with new approaches to build a better organization. The trial-and-error process or occasional rejections will no longer demotivate you, because you will be ready to commit to a stronger, more resilient working system. We will discuss more of this in the next chapter.

7

Be Obsessed with Creating a Robust System

Shift from a person-based mindset to building a systematic workplace.

As someone brought up in a family business, you may have often heard your parents and relatives complain how employees take frequent leaves. Leaves are often correlated with the employee not being serious about their work. Unfortunately, the issue does not lie with the employee. The fact of the matter is that the older generation had spent a lot of time making the business sustainable, and therefore they did not have sufficient time or resources to build a robust, process-driven system. This is not their fault, because they built the family business from scratch and took painstaking efforts to develop things that you and I take for granted today.

In their endless pursuit of profitability, they have depended on a set of dedicated individuals who have believed in their leader and followed their command. However, the business is now established, stable and in motion. It now requires transformation to reach the next level. Dependency on individuals may lead to inefficient working environments and can in turn cause resentment. Employees who grew with the older generation and worked tirelessly to bring the business to its current level often look down upon new team members who take leaves for personal reasons. These newcomers may be serious about their work, but they are not taken seriously due to the perceived notion that responsible employees do not take leaves.

Times are changing and work–life balance is a reality. You want work–life balance, your friends want work–life balance; so, why can't your employees want the same? You may have read various articles on the importance of work–life balance and agreed with their arguments, but perhaps you also feel that these things just sound good on paper, especially for small and medium enterprises in the Indian context. I felt the same way once. However, what we need to understand is that empowering our employees to take leaves and maintain a work–life balance ultimately benefits the company.

The moment you move from a person-dependent organization to a systems-based organization is when you realize that every job role can be defined. In fact, this may seem like a fairly easy thing to do, but I assure you, it's not. Let us do an activity. Try asking your senior managers to define their own job roles, and you will realize there is a lot of vagueness in their descriptions. Their work often overlaps across different departments, and they don't exactly have specific job roles. They are excellent at managing problems and building personal rapport with customers and authorities, but they lack the skillset to structure and define job responsibilities. This is because they have been used to working without clear boundaries. This process has enabled them to outperform others when the company was still finding its feet.

Now that your company is established and requires a structured roadmap to transform into a great enterprise, you will realize that the senior managers need to go through a transformative change as well. When asked to specify their job roles, many will feel confused or even resistant. These are activities no one has made them do before, and this is something out of their comfort zone. Tell them to power through a project by working 12 hours a day, and they would happily do this for you. This is because they are emotionally connected with the business and the family members. In fact, senior employees are the biggest assets of the company due to their unwavering loyalty and belief in their business. However, as your business transforms itself to reach new heights, those very strengths can become obstacles if not checked at the right time.

Let me explain this further. An organization in its early stages of development requires individuals who go out of their way to achieve results. Structures often overlap and responsibilities are not clearly defined. Certain misdemeanours may be overlooked if the individual is performing efficiently and achieving in their respective areas. As the organization starts growing and employs a varied set of individuals, roles and responsibilities need to be clearly defined. Otherwise, we may observe a power structure that is highly skewed in favour of those employees who are closest to the family members.

In 2016, I began a formal project to define the roles and responsibilities of all our employees. This process was done in consultation with an industrial psychologist. First, I communicated the importance of this project to my family members. They were initially confused and wondered why we needed to spend time on this activity. I listened to their concerns and explained to them how creating a clearly defined document for each employee would help us understand the productivity of each individual and enable us to evaluate whether our human resources are being used effectively. After a few rounds of discussions, my family members, although not fully convinced, asked me to proceed with this project with the hope that it would help the organization in the long run. Thus began our project, which on paper appeared quite simple.

We analysed the roles of each employee and simply put it on paper. Once this was done, we handed them the role sheet and personally interacted with each of them. What followed was a period of discomfort. Senior employees were worried what was going on and whether they would be losing their authority. In truth, the document had nothing to do with authority or restructuring anyone's role. All it did was lay down the roles and responsibilities as per the management's understanding.

The thing is that, in family businesses, a lot of things get done verbally. People are hired based on verbal recommendations and instructions are passed down in the same manner. This may save time in the short run, but becomes quite costly in the long run. In case of disputes or confusion, everything comes down to one person's word against another's. Similarly, responsibilities too were rarely documented, leading newcomers to believe that certain senior employees had more authority than they actually did. Once the responsibilities were clearly laid out, we found that not only did it remove ambiguity, it became easier to do performance appraisals as well.

Let us take a simple example of doing performance appraisal for a newcomer. As the business owner, you have probably interacted with this newcomer only three to four times a year, and you are not really sure what their work is. That's because you never really set a roles-and-responsibilities sheet for this newcomer. So, how do you get the performance appraisal completed? Well of course, you call your senior manager and take their views.

This is the first mistake. To be clear, I am not saying that you should not take the senior manager's feedback. The problem is that if your sole metric for performance appraisal is someone's views, then unfortunately you can never create a work environment that is unbiased. Even if the newcomer is extremely hard-working, and even if the senior genuinely like them, a bad day at the office could colour the senior's response. As human beings, we are not rational at all times, and we all have subconscious bias. Therefore, it is imperative that you do not solely rely on the senior's feedback when reviewing anyone at the workplace.

Now let us look at the same example in a different manner. What if you had laid down the roles and responsibilities of the newcomer? If you did that, you could question the senior manager on certain metrics to understand why they like a certain person and why they don't. You would most likely also have a responsibility sheet for the senior manager to gauge how well they have trained the newcomer. Suddenly, you are surrounded by new information that is empowering. A clearly laid out roles-and-responsibilities sheet ensures that you at least have an outline of what you are doing. Without it, quite frankly, you are blind. And as the new generation in the family business who has the responsibility to transform the work environment, you cannot afford to be blind. You may still make two correct decisions out of three, but you are relying on luck as you don't have the data.

Creating a robust system will also promote accountability. Structured systems ensure that managers and employees do not have the scope to 'manage situations'. An experienced professional had once remarked that in our country, senior employees (the ones working for over 20 years) may not be subject matter experts but they are extremely efficient in managing situations. When it comes to resolving an issue by pleading to authorities or finding the right source to jump the queue, they are simply outstanding! These characteristics do work in the company's favour from time to time, but we cannot make this a habit. A robust system has transparency at its core. Organizations with a structured system in place do not need to rely on multiple rounds of investigations, followed by conducting multiple personal hearings of different employees to pinpoint how an error took place. Technology and organized data points do this job for them.

By following the procedural steps of how a job was executed, we assign roles to the concerned persons. Whenever a service failure takes place, systems can pinpoint the exact step where the error took place. This helps us in providing guidance and imparting training to the person who requires it the most. It also creates a culture of accepting responsibility and understanding that the age-old workaround of passing the blame is no longer going to work in your family business. Employees must take responsibility for their role in executing a job, and the management saves crucial time by promptly getting to the crux of the problem.

One of the biggest advantages of a robust system is that employees become aware of how they add value to the organization they work in. A major reason for low job satisfaction is the employee not having a clue how their work contributes to the organization's goals. It is convenient to say that all job roles are important but to inculcate a sense of professional drive in the workplace, employees must be aware of the impact their work creates each day. When employees start working systematically and follow systematic procedures, they see where their role fits within the larger operations. This helps create a sense of commitment as they now realize that the organization's work cannot reach its completion until their task is complete. In a manual unorganized setup this cannot be gauged. Employees may continue working on spreadsheets for long hours and filing reports without understanding how it is adding value to the company's mission statement. They get reprimanded when their work is not up to the mark, but they often get no feedback when they are working well. Moreover, they do not have a clear idea on how their report is being used to add value to the company's service offering.

A systematic method of working begins with explaining the role of each department and each employee within that department. Structures are clearly laid out to ensure stopgaps and to promote learning across different functions. Employees no longer get stuck doing the same job for months and years. It is much easier to shift job roles within an organization as the training is uniform. This opportunity to shift job roles within an organization keeps employees motivated and makes them realize that there are ample opportunities to grow in your family business setup. An organized workplace enables a centralized system where parameters are set for creating reports, filling data, forwarding information to concerned persons and generating reports. This process helps minimize inconsistencies every time an employee leaves the company and is replaced by a newcomer.

You wouldn't like going to a restaurant where the taste of the food changes whenever a particular chef is on leave, would you? You wouldn't like to have a completely different experience when watching a movie in the same multiplex but in a different city. Consistency matters, and yet in most organizations there is a break in consistency when a particular employee is absent or when that employee leaves the organization. It is true that we cannot completely replace a person because each employee has their individual personality and characteristics. However, we can ensure consistent delivery of service by having uniform systems in place where all employees must follow standard operating procedures.

Yes, creating a functioning system will take a lot of time and effort. There would be several moments when one would feel that the process is not worth it. In fact, when I started creating a digital infrastructure with set parameters, we faced various service failures as employees were accustomed to working manually without much reliance on integrated digital tools. Adapting to a digital system felt like going one step forward and two steps back. Yet, we persisted and pushed through the process. That is because we had the end goal in mind. An organization cannot transform itself by solely relying on the hard work of certain individuals. There needs to be a system in place that can spot talented individuals working at the ground level and create a process with transparency at its core. Today, we have enhanced our turnovers while reducing overtime costs. We are more productive, and our departments work in a more synchronized manner. To achieve results and to transform the culture of your family business, the relentless obsession of a youngster will come in handy. In the Industry 4.0 era, digitalization is no longer optional. And so, creating a robust system must be your priority.

In this chapter, I have talked about being *obsessed* with creating a robust system. Now, obsession is not generally perceived to be a positive word. However, I have intentionally used this word because when someone is really dedicated towards a particular pursuit, their focus may look 'obsessive' to the world. The goal here is to be unwaveringly committed to the idea. Once you take the initiative to create a robust system and get more people invested in this idea, it becomes equally important to stay committed to the process and to not drop the idea at the first sign of discomfort. Course corrections are always recommended based on feedback, but conviction comes first. I am not suggesting a rigid approach with no room for changes, but it is important to be convinced with the need for a system. And once you are convinced, you must follow through for the long term and continue improving it each day.

To my reader: List three benefits your organization could gain by developing a robust system where performance is analysed through data. Once you have noted these down, I suggest you keep this at the front of your mind and re-evaluate how daily operations are performed in your company. It is crucial to analyse how data is maintained, what are the stopgaps in place if there is an emergency, how quick your company is in responding to its customers and whether there are clearly defined processes to understand each department's role. Creating a robust system is not a one-time activity. It begins with selecting one area and consistently expanding to cover the entire organizational landscape. In fact, consistency is key to creating a robust system—and I will talk more about this in the next chapter.

8

Accept That There Is Only One Magic Formula—Consistency

Think long term and stay committed to your organization's goals.

We have been subconsciously exposed to the family business from a very young age. We have heard our parents, uncles and extended family members discussing important business matters at the dinner table. As children, we were often clueless regarding the contents of these discussions, which seemed complicated. Our mindset begins to take shape during our teenage years, a period often marked by a 'rebel' phase. During this time, we tend to feel that we have answers to every question. Many of us enter the family business with this mindset, believing that we already have the solutions and know how to take things to the next level. Now don't get me wrong, this can actually be a good thing. The passion and drive to push boundaries are often what motivate young entrepreneurs when they join their family businesses.

Yet, why do most people lose steam during the initial few years? I often discuss this with my peers only to find out a common story: they entered the business with a certain vision, but they gave up on it because things were not moving as fast as they had hoped.

This brings me to a very important principle in both our personal and professional lives—the importance of 'consistency'. Now, being consistent is widely preached. We admire sportspersons who give consistent performances, we like to invest in stocks that give consistent returns, we prefer to drive cars that give consistent mileage, and everyone loves those actors who consistently deliver hit after hit at the box office. Yet, it is not easy to be consistent.

To begin with, business owners often find it boring to be consistent. We have grown up idolizing heroes who came out of nowhere to save the day. In the social media world, where we have the urge to quickly swipe through a 30-second video if the first few seconds are not interesting enough, it's easy to fall for the 'quick hits' trap—the trap of aiming for overnight success, the trap of posting content to get more likes than our friends, the trap of giving up things if they do not work out the first or second time around.

A much tougher task is to look within and find our purpose. I have often mentioned in our company events that it is boring to hear successful people speak. Well, that is because most of them talk about the same thing. They discuss how they stayed on their path despite various adversities and ended up achieving success through sheer perseverance. This doesn't sound complicated but if doing what they did was so easy, then everyone could have been successful. But we all know that is not the case. Consistency is what differentiates successful people from others who had a lot of potential but could not take things to the next level.

Now, here is the paradox. My book is asking you, the

reader, to *change* the status quo. So, how can I advocate *consistency*? Well, the answer is simple. Consistency does not mean simply following what is being done for generations. It means that once you have set your vision, you show up every day and walk on the path that will lead to its fulfilment.

I will give a small example here. In our family business, employees have been working for several years. When I joined the company, I sought assistance from my sister, and together we introduced an 'Employee Felicitation Programme'. We set aside a day to recognize employees across different categories, with the aim of motivating the team and making them feel valued. It would also help us formally recognize employee contributions. Now, when we started this event for the first time in 2015, there was confusion all around. In fact, many employees were scared of what was going to happen. It was something unknown and people seemed quite anxious thinking what would happen during this entire event. Our first Employee Felicitation Programme was awkward to say the least! We did not have a formal script, and we did not even have a good system in place to select the winners. The event left our employees more puzzled rather than motivated. There were two options—either never have this event again or stay consistent to the vision and improve upon the event. I definitely do not refer to consistency as repeating a bad thing. I refer to consistency as a commitment to one's vision. Our vision was to formally recognize our hard-working employees and to create an atmosphere where people would feel valued. Yes, we didn't quite succeed in our first attempt, but we did not give up.

We kept hosting the event each year and it kept getting better with everyone's feedback. In 2025, our ceremony had over 175 employees (compared to 30 employees who attended in 2015) and we also had over 25 long-term clients gracing the event. There were music performances, self-written poetry recitations and TED-talk style speeches on topics such as workplace culture. Awards were given based on 360-degree feedback taken from over 100 employees at various locations and even our valued clients attended the event. Our clients were amazed to see a company in the MSME sector pull off such a grand employee felicitation. In fact, some of them were convinced that this grand celebration was organized by an outsourced event-management team! This was definitely not the case, and since 2015, we have been organizing our employee felicitation ceremony consistently with our in-house team who have followed a script that has evolved over the past decade. We are closer to our vision now than we were in 2015, and this was only possible due to consistency. Often, we end up stopping initiatives and programmes based on one bad experience. It is really important during these unfavourable moments to remember the vision and the reason why we started the initiative in the first place.

If we look closely at big organizations and big projects, we will notice the word 'consistency' screaming at us from all angles. What appears magical from a distance is nothing more than consistent production of effort over a sustained period of time when inspected from close quarters. Your family business has reached its current level due to consistent efforts of your family members, and we must always respect this. If you do decide to take things forward, then, having first made sure you understand the business, begin by taking up small projects within the organization. Think long and hard what objective you wish to achieve through these projects and commit to them. At times, your office days may feel mundane, and the project may get stuck. Do remember to brainstorm and always recall the reason why you started. It will help you stay on track and motivate you to consistently show up to complete your project. After executing a series of projects, you will start understanding your family business in a much better manner. You will also find inspiration from within, seeing how your small projects are adding to the bigger picture of transforming your family business.

Consistency should not be confused with stubbornness. Some people are consistent at sticking to their strategies even if there is overwhelming evidence that the approach is not yielding desirable results. This is why it's important to first know what you really want for your family business. If your goal is transformational growth for your business, you must have the right structures in place—a good business plan, a product or service people want and systematic processes. You cannot consistently work 15 hours a day and expect success without sound foundations.

Once the basics are in place, you need to understand how you would like your workplace to be. Is it a place where people enjoy working or is it a place where people can't wait to return home? You need to introspect how you want your own family business to be perceived. Do you want it to look like a professional organization or a place where family members are never held accountable for errors? It is crucial to think deeply about these questions before committing to a vision. If questions arise, do discuss with your family members, consultants and colleagues, and get clarity. Setting the future of your family business requires constant dialogue with the important stakeholders. Once there is clarity and a vision is set, one that you truly believe in, get to work and be consistent in your efforts to bring that vision to reality.

I am from the logistics industry. Some of you may be from the hotel, finance, manufacturing, IT, insurance, mental health, event management, or other completely different sectors. The formula remains the same across all industries. We face different types of challenges each day, and as our business grows, we come across problems we did not even know existed. How can we tackle these challenges without a consistent business philosophy, a consistent drive to follow the company's vision and mission statement, a consistent pledge to build upon the company's key value drivers? Earlier in my book, I talked about creating a mission statement for the company—and this is something that is crucial. But once that mission statement has been set up, we must commit to following the template consistently.

With changing market dynamics, we can alter our marketing strategies, our recruitment strategies, job roles of key personnel, client retention policies, operational techniques, etc. Change is a necessity for growth. However, in today's changing environment it is more important than ever to have a consistent commitment towards your organization's mission statement. We are observing various companies having identity crisis where people do not recognize what the company stands for anymore. It's not that these companies are not profitable, but the problem is that their loyal customers can no longer connect with the company's values. Yes, the rewards are great in the short term as they keep capitalizing on every new trend, but after a few years when these companies look back, the top management often feels that they lost sight of the bigger picture. Committing to consistency will help resist temptations of quick fixes and short-term growth prospects, keeping you firmly on the path to sustained success.

You could be doing many other things in your life, but you have made a conscious decision to join your family business. Okay, perhaps at some point you felt you didn't really have a choice when it came to selecting your professional career. You can narrate whatever story you would like to yourself, and that again is completely your choice. The truth is that, at this moment in time, as you read this book, you are actively choosing to continue working in your family business.

So, how can you add value to the business? How can you go home and feel that you are not simply going through the motions and living in your comfort zone? The answer lies in figuring out what makes you show up to work each day. If you don't get the answer, then keep looking and keep creating an environment that enables you to be passionate about your family business. It won't happen in a day; it may take years. However, one day you will find that staying 'consistent' to your vision during times of uncertainty and self-doubt will shape you as an individual and, in turn, transform your organizational culture. This all begins with the acceptance that you—yes you, the individual—have the power to make a difference.

Consistently performing small yet meaningful activities every single day adds to the bigger picture and leads to a major change over a period of time. I have a funny example of how a small consistent change led to a positive health impact in our organization. In India, we are aware that most people have a sweet tooth, and they do not like to compromise on their afternoon tea, which is usually loaded with sugar. We once had a health drive in our organization where a nutritionist mentioned the negative impact of adding white sugar to our beverages. While our employees acknowledged this, they could not imagine having tea without sugar during their office breaks. A family member then came up with an idea where they encouraged our employees to not stop having sugar with their tea but to reduce from two sugar sachets to one.

Most employees felt this was a better alternative to having tea without sugar but wondered what difference one less sachet could make, and that they might as well continue their old habit of having tea loaded with two or at times even three sachets of sugar. This is where the compounding aspect of consistent behaviour comes in. That family member pointed out that by reducing just one sachet of sugar in tea, the employees would be reducing two sachets of sugar intake each day (as most employees would drink tea at least twice a day), which would lead to at least 10 sachets less a week and 40 sachets less a month. That's 480 sachets less a year. It sounds huge when you look back—480 less sachets of sugar consumed in a year—but at a micro level, it is just one small choice each day. Small, consistent actions add up to create big meaningful changes.

Yes, when we admire big companies with their wonderful state-of-the-art systems and excellent work culture, it is important to remember that they too started with that one small yet meaningful change consistently built upon over time.

The only magic formula in our personal and professional lives is consistency. It may sound boring, but consistency means doing what others don't want to, so that your company can develop a culture others do not have. Today's world is full of flashy advertisements and influencers promoting a false notion of getting instant success by doing something extraordinary. We find these messages exciting, and they make us question whether our path is worth taking. Let me assure you, real success and transformational growth will only come if you are consistent in following your company's core values.

> **To my reader:** Think of an activity that needs to be performed consistently for your organization to grow. It could be something like visiting at least two key clients a week or attending one training or workshop a month. Analyse whether this activity is being done and if yes, check whether the frequency of this activity is being maintained. This will enable you to track the consistency levels. There would be people who may question you or raise doubts about why you are focusing on tasks that seem insignificant at a macro level. But you have to stick to your vision. Sometimes, the people questioning you could be your own family members, and you will need tact and emotional intelligence to deal with them. In the next chapter, we will explore how to deal with these situations with balance and understanding.

9

Regulating Emotions During Situations of Conflict

Respect the process of building relations with family members.

As a youngster in the family business, there are a lot of people looking at you to take the business to the next level. Senior family members, siblings, college friends, even your house staff who has seen you since a young age—everyone is interested to know how you will develop your family business. Advice may also come from different quarters on which areas you must focus on. If you feel things are getting overwhelming, then you are not alone. A lot of youngsters have felt the same and many have unfortunately quit the family business setup due to unrealistic expectations from senior family members. Therefore, it is very important for you to take things at your own pace and build something often ignored in the Indian family business context—emotional intelligence.

I regularly interact with people who are also working in a family business setup. It was an eye-opening experience to hear from one of my friends that apart from senior family members, he also had to work with his elder brother who joined the business a few years before him. Now, the elder brother had always seen him as the younger sibling and taken care of him. Therefore, during family board meetings, my friend would often have issues opening up and sharing his opinions, especially when he wanted the business to take a different direction than the one proposed by his elder brother. He would appear frustrated because his views were evaluated less on their merits and more on his status as the youngest member in the family business. Hearing his experiences made me realize the importance of addressing this dynamic in the family business—something not discussed often. While talking about the need to professionalize the work environment and create a robust structure, it is crucial to also emphasize the importance of dealing with family members who belong to the same generation as us.

The above example of conflict amongst siblings may or may not have been relatable to you. If you have not experienced the above, you may have at least heard from your parents, especially your father, how tough it was to manage business and personal relations with their own siblings. Family business is tough and through this book, I want to share my personal experiences, which will help you become better equipped in dealing with such situations.

In our family business, I have also grown up seeing conflicts between my father and my uncle. I was lucky enough to see them look beyond their differences and work towards a common goal of taking the business to greater heights. But we all know that this is not always the case. Often, thriving family businesses split because differences between family members become so great that they are unable to function as a unit.

It is fair to say that you will also have your share of conflicts with family members. So, what can you do to ensure that you are able to implement your learnings and take your family business to the next level without severing personal relations with your relatives? Yes, you know what I am going to say by now. The answer is to build your emotional intelligence. So, let us talk about this.

Encyclopaedia Britannica defines emotional intelligence as:

> A set of psychological faculties that enable individuals to perceive, understand, express, and control their emotions and to discern and respond appropriately to the emotions of others.

Let us break this down in simpler terms with an activity. Think of an incident where you had a heated argument with someone. That someone could be your parents, your spouse, your relative, your best friend or even a complete stranger on the road. Close your eyes and revisit the incident for a couple of minutes. How did this activity of revisiting the moment make you feel? Did you feel anger, regret, anxiousness or any other such emotions? Chances are that you did not really remember the incident on the basis of merit or evaluate who was right or wrong. Instead, you probably recalled the emotional toil that the argument had on you.

When you look back at unpleasant moments, you realize that the outcome hardly matters. Yes, at that moment we all want to shout our lungs out and prove that we are right. We want to, for lack of a better word, defeat the other person with our facts and figures, but when we look back after a passage of time, we realize that no one really wins in such situations.

Upon reflection, do you feel that the situation wouldn't have escalated if you had just taken a deep breath instead of getting triggered by certain words mentioned by the other person during that argument? I am not saying that it is your fault that the situation got escalated, but what I am advocating for is to become aware of your triggers and to create strategies to regulate your responses. During tense situations and times of conflict, it is important to observe our emotions instead of reacting spontaneously and escalating the matter. This is what is meant by emotional intelligence. Yes, what I am talking about is definitely easier said than done, but that is the goal if you truly want to take your family business to the next level.

It is you who is reading this book and learning some new concepts with it, but you may be wondering how it could help you in dealing with those family members who have not studied management theories and have instead only implemented policies based on practical knowledge. It all begins with asking questions. Some questions that have helped me develop good interpersonal relations with family members are:

- Where would you like to see our business in the next five years?
  (*It makes them feel valued that you want their opinion on how the family business should grow in the future.*)
- When you were building the business, what is one area where you wished you had received more support from your family members?

(*It makes them feel heard that someone wants to know their story of struggle.*)

- Are you happy that I have taken the decision to invest my time and effort in building the business?

  (*It makes them feel happy that you care about their views.*)
- What would I need to do to make you trust my decision-making ability?

  (*It makes them feel respected that you want to earn their trust.*)

Questions are important because they help the senior members of the family business as well as your own siblings to open up. When you are asking a question, you are making the other person feel valued.

Now if you rearrange the above questions into statements, you will notice how the same words could cause your family members to become defensive. Let us try it; let us change the above questions to statements from your perspective as a youngster:

- My vision for this family business in the next 5 years is…

  (*It makes them feel you are not taking their inputs into account when planning the future of the family business—one in which they have invested so much time and effort.*)
- I want to get more support from my family members in the following areas…

  (*It makes them feel they are not being valued for the support and facilities they are already providing to you.*)
- I have taken such a big step in investing my time and efforts to grow this family business…

  (*It makes them feel you are taking the business and its current position for granted.*)

- I have studied at a reputed university, which makes me capable to take decisions regarding...
  (*It makes them feel that you are showing arrogance for your education, which they have paid for through hard work and perseverance.*)

The tone of the above statements makes family members defensive because they are being communicated from a self-centric point of view. Emotional intelligence is giving your family members the respect and opportunity to express their opinions to you.

Yes, you may be thinking about that one family member who would not give a straight answer to your question and perhaps even make you feel demotivated. But let us not assume already. Give them the opportunity to respond to your questions instead of always sharing where you want to take the business and expecting automatic support. Perhaps, you will learn a few interesting points through these questions, and they would appreciate your inquisitiveness to hear from their experiences. Such dialogues led by inquisitive questions will help you build a strong bond with your family members and make them realize that you are no longer that young kid, but a grown up, responsible individual who cares about the opinions of others.

As you grow and scale the family business, be rest assured that there will be times of intense conflict. Tempers will rise and relations will get strained due to decisions taken at work. In such moments, the response should neither be to react angrily and sever all ties nor be submissive and give up your vision just to maintain peace. Instead, engage through questions like:

- If you see me do something you don't like but you realize that I am passionate about my vision, what can I do to maintain amicable relations with you?
- If our visions are diverging, how do you propose we reach a common ground, since both of us want to take the family business forward?
- Would you be open to revisiting this conversation after we both have taken some time to evaluate each other's points?
- Do you feel we can communicate on this topic without resorting to personal attacks?

Questions like these enable family members to take a pause and get out of the competitive mindset: 'for me to win, you have to lose'. Clarity and respect are essential when dealing with conflict amongst family members. It is quite unfortunate many family business houses fail due to bitterness amongst relatives. In fact, the bitterness sometimes gets to such a point where they are ready to cause damage to themselves just to harm the other.

You, the next generation of the family business, must focus on creating an environment where senior members believe in win–win scenarios. It would surely take time and a lot of patience, but nothing sustainable was built overnight. It is easier to launch yourself in an attack mode to prove a point, only to gradually see an invisible wall between you and your siblings or senior family members. It is not worth it to win an argument in the short run and lose trust in the long run. The process of intentionally building a long-term relation with family members will lead to manifold benefits over the years and decades.

During my initial years in our family business, we were facing some labour-related issues at one of our sites. The issue had been persisting for several years, and many senior employees had given lofty commitments to our family members, assuring them that they would solve the matter in a few weeks, only to make it worse. The issue was that they underestimated the unity of the workers' union and more importantly, they focused on delaying the problems instead of resolving them. They looked down upon any worker who was a part of the workers' union, considering them disloyal.

When I got involved in the matter, I realized that it needed to be handled delicately. There were various unreasonable demands from the workers' union but some of their requirements appeared genuine. When I suggested that we hear them out, because perhaps we could learn a thing or two on how we could improve, the senior employees were shocked. To them, any worker associated with the union could not be trusted.

After some discussions with the workmen and our managers, I realized that we needed professional help from a legal counsel. The counsel guided us on how to professionalize our work systems to ensure that senior managers were not blatantly favouring those workers who were not a part of the union. The legal counsel mentioned that our company must have a uniform system where the processes are clearly defined and workmen are aware of the criteria for overtime, leaves, attendance and the possibility of receiving show-cause letters in case they had breached the company's code of conduct.

When we started the process of creating these policies, there was resistance from the senior employees. They firmly believed that they had worked so hard for so many years to somehow manage the issue of the workers' union, and now suddenly, a new approach was being taken where worker grievances were also being heard. I used to have discussions with my father on this matter who was initially not convinced with the way things were going. There were important discussions at home on whether I, as the next generation, should involve myself in such a 'petty' matter instead of focusing on business growth.

Although I was convinced that I needed to get the basics right before thinking of scaling up our operations, I did not approach these discussions with my father with an intention to convince him. I engaged in dialogue through questions.

I asked him whether this union issue was a nuisance that was affecting his peace of mind. He agreed but mentioned that these issues may never be resolved and could even worsen over time despite my intervention. I acknowledged his concerns and asked him how much time he was willing to give me if I really wanted to work on this issue. He thought about my question, and after various discussions and upon hearing my strategies and plan of action, he told me to try my best for the next six months. And if things had not changed by then, I would focus my attention elsewhere.

This proposal seemed reasonable, and I agreed. During the next six months, we made steady progress and saw a rare improvement in the relationships between management and workers. This gave my dad the confidence in my approach to deal with the union. We started creating better systems, and now it's been over 10 years that our site is working on 24/7 basis without any union-related interruptions. I am not saying that we don't face any problems or grievances anymore, but now we have a structure in place to address them.

I don't believe this would have been possible if I had

tried to just push my way through my status as the next generation family business owner. I had to take things slow, hear the inputs of my senior employees and earn their trust as well. I made considerable efforts to communicate to them that the company appreciates their loyalty and their years or service. But if someone else does not show the same attributes, then it doesn't make them a bad person. It simply means that we all have our own unique qualities, and we must focus on having harmonious relations with workers who are on site, whether in heat, rain or cold, to ensure our operations run seamlessly.

I had to give my senior employees the benefit of the doubt as well because they had grown up in a different era and they were too scared to take a decision that could negatively impact the organization. So delaying matters seemed the best option for them.

Looking back, I realize how important it was to communicate with people and make them feel heard. It enabled me to bring a sustainable change in our workplace dynamics.

To my reader: Can you think of an issue related to your family business that often gets discussed at home? Do you feel you could offer a different perspective on resolving that issue but you refrain from sharing it for fear it may not be well-received or could create conflict in the future? Now that you understand the importance of engaging in dialogues through questions, could you try this new approach to have meaningful conversations with your family members? Reflect on this and take an initiative to engage in such question-oriented conversations on a regular basis with both family members and employees. When doing so, always be intentional and remember that you have the power to make a difference. I will discuss more on this in the next chapter.

10

Remember that You Have the Power to Make a Difference

Take ownership of your actions and initiate changes to transform the business.

We all seek the power to make a difference. Many of us crave the power to command a room full of attentive listeners. Some of us hope to be the most powerful person in any room we walk into. Yet, we are often resigned to the fact that our time may not have come yet.

This is indeed true for youngsters joining their legacy family businesses. Most of us enter with a mindset to test out the waters and wait till we are ready with all facts, figures, operational knowledge, marketing knowhow, and relevant business acumen before making key decisions. This isn't really a bad thing. But I have previously mentioned that while it is important to know the ethos of your family business before initiating change, it is equally important to not remain stuck.

At times, youngsters resign to notions that they are not taken seriously and their opinions are not valued, and therefore cannot make much of a difference in their family business. This is common in most family businesses. Our elders have built the business from scratch, and they are very passionate about each and every aspect of the organization. Their reservations may prevent them from acting upon each idea delivered by the young entrant. We cannot control how others feel; no amount of reading or preparation will give us the power to dictate someone else's emotions. What we can instead focus on is making small yet impactful steps in our business.

For example, when I entered my family business I approached it with a similar mindset. I was learning the business dynamics from a comfortable seat, and I felt that I could only make a meaningful impact once I know the entire operations. The reality is that I was trying to avoid making any mistakes, and I was using the guise of perfectionism to procrastinate decision making. After a few months, I realized that I was not really going to make any positive contributions if I just sat back and kept analysing business activities. I needed to break the complex operations into smaller processes and make those value additions that I deemed fit.

Initially, I started with something that appeared to be a very small step at that time. I realized that our management team was so focused on increasing the business turnover and operational efficiency that we had not really taken time to revamp our company's visiting cards. I felt our company could do with a redesigned visiting card. Yes, there may be an opinion somewhere that this is too small a thing for a business owner to think about. Perhaps that is true but for me it felt like a good point to start.

So, as I started redesigning the visited card, I thought about the certifications that we should display on it which would truly showcase our company's brand value. This led to me studying about the different certifications we had, which in turn motivated me to understand the processes that we follow to maintain these certifications and how we can further improve upon them. I also started researching new certifications that would add to our company's branding. The initial redesign was not really a groundbreaking shift from the existing one, but after a few drafts, we came up with a design that was crisp and stood out as unique.

A small start led to a snowball effect and it opened up various new pathways for me. Looking back, it was always the easier choice to sit back and realize that I may be 'too cool' for these activities. After all, designing a visiting card is not something people talk about as their contributions. The thing is—this activity made me realize that starting something is better than going nowhere and sitting behind the comfort of being a newcomer who is simply understanding how things work.

Time doesn't wait for anyone; if you feel intimidated by your family business and worry about how you could make an impact, well, start small. No one can lift a 50 kg dumbbell on their first day. There are people who want to get fit but never visit the gym because they are too intimidated by the fancy equipment and the people there. Similarly, youngsters joining the family businesses also feel anxious as people begin to have expectations from them as soon as they join. It's okay for others to have expectations, and it's completely okay to not know how to devise solutions to complex problems from the get-go. Just remember that the person who is a professional weightlifter was once an amateur who simply showed up every day. Once we accept that we have the power to make a difference, we start looking at the world in a different light.

When I look back, the simple step of redesigning my company's visiting card led me to review our certifications and made me look for other accreditations that may add value to our family business. This modest activity, which planted an idea in 2015, led our company to become the first MSME Indian logistics organization with its head office in Kolkata to become 'Great Place to Work' certified by Great Place to Work®, India, in the year 2019.

The power to make a difference. Heavy words, for sure! If a business owner came up with a strategy that completely transformed the company's trajectory and quadrupled the annual turnover, did they make a difference? Yes! If a business owner understood the reason why a data entry operator was not performing up to the mark and tweaked the work environment to positively add value to the data entry operator's work ethic, did they make a difference? Yes, they did too! The impact of the difference may vary but, in both scenarios, we cannot deny that a meaningful difference was made.

The starting point of accepting that you can make a difference is to realize that making small yet meaningful changes matter. Yes, everyone wants to find that illusive strategy that can quadruple growth. I completely get that. However, the point here is to not keep our professional life on hold till we find that because, let's face it, there is a strong chance we may not. What we can control is showing up each day consistently knowing that we have the power to make this a good day for our organization, our employees, our family members and ourselves.

What if you went back home every Saturday and thought about the positive contributions you made to the organization the past week? The moment you ask this to yourself, you will turn your focus to the activities performed that have created a sustainable change, no matter how small that change may be. I firmly believe that a revolutionary transformation is nothing more than a series of small yet effective changes that have been consistently executed over time.

Suppose you are looking to make a change, but you strongly feel your dad may not accept it. You are not comfortable communicating this with him, and hence the idea is put on hold indefinitely. If you have a series of ideas that you are not able to execute due to this reason, then it's understandable that you feel demotivated. Words in this book may seem nice to hear but they may not really be practical for you.

I have a suggestion. Think of that idea you really want to execute but you feel you don't have the courage to bring it up with your dad or a senior family member. How about you take it down a notch and first conceive an idea that *you* find doable, something that you can bring up with your family members more comfortably? We sometimes need to start from one step below before we can reach our desired goal.

What if that idea is heard and appreciated but shut down? Once again, there are two options. Resign yourself to the fact that no one takes you seriously, or think of an even smaller idea that may be communicated and have a slightly higher chance of getting accepted?

You see, we are approaching the entire situation now with a conscious acceptance that we have the power to make a difference. Therefore, we will lower our expectations and go for a smaller win. Soon, we start noticing that by at least getting the smaller wins, we are no longer remaining stuck. Our family members sooner or later will start appreciating our perseverance, and in a few months, or in some cases a few years, you will start gratefully accepting that you indeed have the power to make a difference.

Just because a farmer doesn't have the power to create rainfall doesn't make them useless. It just means the farmer needs to focus more on the things in their control, right? Similarly, just because you may not currently have the power to make the top-level policy decisions, it doesn't mean that you are only expected to sit around and complain about life being unfair. You can rise to the challenge by setting small yet meaningful daily targets to accomplish.

One of the most interesting things I hear when talking to my peers is how in our generation, we simply don't have enough time! 'Yes, we want to make a lot of changes but how can we do so many things in one day? During our parents' time, there was no Netflix, Spotify or Amazon. They had more time to follow their passion.'

Well, I won't deny that when I joined the business, I thought about these things as well. For example, I am an avid video gamer who used to daydream about which game I'm going to play at night while sitting in the office. I would feel passionate about starting something, but then I would realize that this process would take a lot of time, and I would have to sacrifice my hobbies. We all have gone through this, and honestly, we will always have this problem. In such cases, it helps to accept reality. Yes, time is indeed limited. We cannot do 200 things in a day, and that's when it becomes important to prioritize. What if I change the narrative from 'I don't have time to do that project' to 'That project is not so important to me that I will spend an extra hour on it.'

Words have a lot of power. The sooner we realize that not having time is simply an excuse, the easier it becomes to accept reality. Yes, life is tough and there are a lot of people who are working very hard to achieve success. Even they have the same 24 hours in a day that we do. It's rather about how they are spending that time. So am I advocating for one to not have a social life and just keep focusing on work all the time? Not at all.

I reiterate what I have written earlier in this book—it is important to have a clear vision. If you don't really have a vision for your family business and you are satisfied with the way things are, that's okay. Just be honest and accept it. It's a difficult pill to swallow but one that would make your life better in the long run. We often give up the power of ownership and simply hand over our life's remote control to others. This is a recipe for disaster because this is the very moment when we start becoming dishonest with our very own selves. Perhaps after self-reflection you may realize that your passion does not lie in your family business but elsewhere.

It may be true that you just don't feel motivated enough to make a difference or to understand the family business in a more holistic manner. If that is the case, you have a choice. Either you show up every day regardless of how you feel for a certain period of time and see if things change, or you give up and do something else that may work out for you. Both options are good. The only option that should not be taken up is to give away your power and say that you don't have the time or resources or that there are too many distractions in the present age to really focus on transforming the business. This is a scenario where neither you nor your family members are going to be happy. The moment we start believing in this excuse that we don't have an option is when we start diminishing our own self-worth.

It's an easy way out to assume that our generation is facing a lot more distractions than the previous one. At the end of the day, each generation has faced their own set of challenges and we must not trivialize their struggles. There are people in the older generation who struggled to focus, just as there are people in our generation who have an eagle eye for identifying their goals and pursuing them. Generalization is often an easy way out when we are intimidated by reality. The reality is that we are scared to accept that we have the freedom to choose. Once we accept this, we will know that we have the power to make a difference and now it is up to us whether we want to use that power or not.

Watching that show on Netflix because all your friends are watching it? That's a choice. Waking up late because all your friends went for that night out and so you had to join them? That's a choice. Not contributing to the workplace because you are distracted by thoughts of spending the evening with your friends? That's a choice. Blaming the traffic for arriving late to work? Yes, that's also a choice. We make hundreds of choices in our daily lives, yet we fail to acknowledge them as choices. Instead, we often act as if we are running on automation and the decisions are being made on our behalf. Knowing that you have the choice to pursue a hobby, the choice to decline a night out, the choice to implement a small initiative, the choice to stay calm even during a chaotic traffic jam, that's the ultimate power.

People who make a difference acknowledge that they have the power to do so. We all have the power to influence our surroundings. As a newcomer joining the family business, you have the power to change the status quo by simply smiling and greeting 'good morning' to your employees who are used to seeing seniors storm into their chambers without greeting anyone. The possibilities are endless once we start recognizing our potential and the impact we can make. This will also help us effectively allocate our time.

I would like to give a personal example here. In my high school days, I was really passionate about learning languages and had diligently studied Spanish. Once I joined college, I said to myself that I simply didn't have the time to pursue this hobby, and this mental scripting got further reinforced once I joined my family business. I did not even touch a Spanish book for years.

One day, I was reflecting on my hobbies and realized that I had just given up the power and made an excuse that I didn't have time. So back in 2018, I made a small habit of studying Spanish 10 minutes a day at night. Yes, just 10 minutes. In fact, there were many days when I could not even allocate those few minutes for this. Yet, I never fully stopped, and I ended up studying Spanish 10 minutes a day for around four days a week. After a few months, I began to make progress and felt increasingly motivated. I gradually increased my practice time to 20 minutes a day, and then to half an hour. In the year 2024, I visited Spain on a vacation and was able to converse with locals in their own language. They were amazed to learn that I had taught myself Spanish with the help of online tutors.

From barely finding even 10 minutes a day to study, I gradually began dedicating almost half an hour every day to this hobby over several years. When I made that small commitment, I did not really know where it would lead me. All I knew was that I could not give my power away by saying, 'I don't have time'. Instead, I had to face reality: *Learning Spanish was clearly not important enough for me to even set aside 10 minutes for it.* That realization held up a mirror to me. So, I started small, and over time the practice grew naturally.

There may be similar instances in your life when you want to do something and then you push it away by saying, 'I don't have the time'. Be honest with yourself and reframe that sentence. I am not saying I would have done anything wrong by admitting that Spanish wasn't important for me. There are many hobbies I have given up because I outgrew them. What I would like the takeaway to be is that the moment we change our mental scripting and start acknowledging that we have the power to make decisions, it has a positive impact on all aspects of our professional and personal lives.

You may find all this motivating and feel inspired to take initiatives once you become aware of the power you hold. As you begin to put your own stamp on things and take ownership, there will be moments when you feel that it was better letting someone else have the remote control. After all, 'ignorance is bliss', and many of our peers find it easier to continue with the status quo. That is completely fine too. See, the choice is yours!

But if your aim is to transform your family business, you must invest time in understanding the present value structure of your company, talking to your seniors about the changes you wish to make, creating a plan on how to implement these changes and then building trust among employees so they align with your vision. None of this is possible till you believe in the potential you possess and wholeheartedly remind yourself that you as an individual have the power to make a difference. This realization will help you not just professionally, but in your personal life as well.

To my reader: Reflect on how you perceive your current family business model. Are there any areas you would like to change? After a thorough introspection, identify the steps you need to take to initiate this change. Once you start acknowledging that you have the power to make a difference, you will value the 24 hours you have each day. You will analyse how you want to allocate your time and begin scheduling activities that are important to you. I will focus on the concept of scheduling activities for enhanced time management in the next chapter.

11

Schedule Your Business Activities

Allocate time for activities that will contribute to your professional and personal growth.

We live life at a frantic pace. From getting ready for a client meeting to making plans for the next vacation to assessing the next possible business project, everything must happen 'now'. We are hooked to the world of unlimited choices, and we want to acquire everything we see around us. We often speak about our ambitions to our friends:

'I want to go to the gym and get fit!

'I want to learn playing the guitar soon.'

'I want to go to a jungle safari this summer.'

'I want to add at least 15 more clients to my portfolio this quarter.'

You get the drift. We talk about our aspirations and our goals in a nonchalant manner. We may come across a new business idea while chatting with friends during an evening catch-up and feel strongly that we have found our calling; yet that unwavering spirit often fizzles out by the very next morning. Why does this happen? I believe that youngsters have a lot of passion to make a difference, but when we sit down and prepare an actual roadmap for the things we need to do in order to reach our goals, we begin to realize the obstacles we would have to overcome. Most of us then become disheartened and start seeking the next interesting idea that would probably not require that much effort. Guess what? That will never happen. Instead, we have to start introspecting and acknowledging the changes we need to make in our lives.

The key to growth and the secret to achieving concrete goals is maintaining a schedule. Yes, scheduling is one of the most important tasks for the next generation youngsters joining the family business. As newcomers, we sometimes get comfortable or rather complacent seeing that we are one of the youngest people in our organization. We start feeling that we have a lot of time to do things, and as a result of that, we tend to go with the flow. We fail to spot the golden opportunity we have right in front of us, which is that we can make an impact from such an early stage in our career.

Of course, there are plenty of youngsters who join the family business with utmost sincerity. It's just that we are not taught the valuable lesson of respecting time. Yes, we do hear from our parents that one should sleep on time and wake up early. Unfortunately, I am the first to admit that I have tried multiple times and failed in my quest to wake up early on a regular basis. In fact, what if I told you that as a family business owner, it doesn't really matter when you wake up? Sounds like I'm one of those entitled youngsters who takes his family business for granted, right?

Well, that's not what I mean to say here. What I would like to emphasize is that waking up early is not going to be relevant if we don't have a schedule. If we are to grow in both our professional and personal lives, we need to first accept that our time is limited in this world. Yes, as youngsters, we often feel we will never grow old, but sadly, that won't be the case. The sooner we start scheduling our tasks, the sooner we will recognize the consistent effort required in order to get closer to our goals and aspirations.

I would suggest creating a schedule at the start of each week. This schedule should not be limited to work but should also include time for your hobbies. For example, let's say you want to learn to play the guitar. In fact, let's say you really, really want to learn to play the guitar! Yet a few months go by, and you realize that you have never even touched your beloved guitar because you have been busy working or partying with your friends. After a year, you just give up and come to the conclusion that running an active family business and pursuing a hobby is simply not possible. It is indeed a comfortable conclusion to reach, but the real reason is that you never really scheduled your task.

Scheduling our activities is not as easy as it may appear. Firstly, I would advise against having a daily schedule, because such a schedule ends up becoming a to-do list. A weekly planner, on the other hand, enables us to get out of the microscopic mindset of completing day-to-day urgent tasks and instead reach our long-term holistic goals by reviewing progress made across different aspects of life during the week. The planner can be made at the start of the week and reviewed at the weekend. Creating a formal schedule may appear challenging at first. After going through different concepts, I ended up creating a weekly schedule format, which looks something like this:

WEEKLY ACTIVITIES: MONDAY TO SUNDAY	
Activity type	**Objectives**
Personal growth	• Have ___ meditative sessions. • Continue reading ___ book.
Family	• Watch a movie with parents. • Go out for dinner with my friend from ___.
Friends/business network	• Attend the ___ business event. • Call friend from high school I haven't spoken to for the last six months.
Team development	• Organize a training session for ___ department.
Company branding	• Execute one Instagram reel and two social media posts for the company.
Work research	• Understand the issue related to ___, which led to a client complaint last month. • Follow up with consultant regarding assessment schedule for managers.

At the end of each week, I review the activities I was able to do and note the activities I couldn't. There are several weeks where I am unable to complete all the activities I had in mind. However, by maintaining a planner, I am able to identify the areas I focused on during the past week, as well as the activities I missed. Reviewing this helps me prepare better for the following week and identify my true priorities.

By dividing our planner into various components and individually filling out activities against each section, we will actually begin to appreciate the importance of time allocation. We will no longer make an excuse that we don't have time, because we will be setting our priorities at the start of each week. All that remains is to review what we accomplished and where we fell short. If certain activities remain unfinished week after week, we can analyse whether time was genuinely lacking or whether that area of interest is simply not a priority. In short, maintaining a weekly planner provides a much-needed reality check on our overall progress and growth.

As a youngster joining the family business, you must be careful not to overlook your overall development. Yes, passion for the business is essential but completely sacrificing your health, hobbies and social circle is not recommended. A planner will help you maintain a healthy balance in the way you are living your life. You will start noticing that you are able to give time to your hobbies, while also focusing on different areas of work. Reviewing your week will give you a sense of accomplishment when you find that you have completed most of your planned activities.

We all hear a great deal about time management and we do understand its importance, but we are unable to truly take control of our time. Time management is not just about consistency or doing the fastest work in the shortest amount of time. At its core, time management is about minimizing procrastination tendencies and allowing yourself to grow without leading an overly stressful life.

And no—you do not need to sacrifice your Netflix show, your video gaming sessions, your movie nights or your social night out with friends! What effective time management does is cut out the excesses. It prompts you to reflect on how you missed out on important hobbies and work-related projects that were planned this week simply because you stayed up the whole night binge watching your favourite TV show. Yes, we all do that at times, but by having a planner, you at least know which activities you missed out on. Awareness is the first step towards effective scheduling. Time is precious and scheduling helps us allocate this resource in a proper manner, rather than looking back with regrets on how we could not pursue things we loved due to a lack of time.

Moreover, scheduling tasks helps us sort out our priorities. We may make casual, lofty claims about wanting to get physically fit while learning golf, playing the guitar, and even participating in a local swimming competition. However, once we get down to scheduling, we may realize that there is just not enough time to manage so many things while being a full-time member of the family business. Scheduling helps us make tough but much-needed choices, and it helps in actually focusing on the hobbies we really want to develop. It's better to spend time effectively learning one or two hobbies, rather than being so overwhelmed with the choices around us that we don't even know where to start.

I would like to highlight here that scheduling does not mean micromanaging each aspect of your life. In fact, it is about devoting time to your work, your personal life, your social circle, as well as pursuing new projects and hobbies. Once we get down to creating a weekly planner, initially it may seem that we are sucking the fun out of our lives. Well, that's because we are finally leaving our dreamland of unlimited choices with zero results and facing the tough reality of having to choose between things we would like to do.

Youngsters joining the family business have heard stories of struggles faced by the previous generation to get the family business to a certain level. They have seen expansion of their family business and the progress that took place in a relatively unorganized manner, compared to the structured growth we see in multinational companies. Yes, your family business has reached this level due to the hard work and toil of your parents, grandparents, uncles and extended family members. However, in order to take the business forward in the Industry 4.0 era, simply working hard is not going to cut it. You must know how effectively you can utilize your working hours.

You will need to maximize the productivity of your company's infrastructure, which includes physical assets, working capital, digital systems, human resources, as well as intellectual properties. To devote adequate attention to various aspects of the business, you must first learn to efficiently allocate your time. Else, you may spend each day firefighting and handling one crisis after another. Without a schedule, you will end up thinking you are doing a lot of work, but you would look back at the end of each quarter realizing that you have not made as much of an impact as you would have liked.

There are some important things to acknowledge when creating a schedule. First, it is essential to realize that you are in a position of privilege to create a schedule for your life. There are many people in this world who are so busy surviving that they cannot really afford to make a productive schedule and think of transformative growth. I have regularly mentioned in my book that joining a family business is a privilege and we must realize this privilege to make the most out of this opportunity.

By creating a schedule, you are focusing on things that are important but may not require urgent attention. Yes, that interest to learn the guitar can wait, that desire to visit the gym can wait, that jungle safari trip can wait too. Such activities are surely not urgent matters needing to be attended to immediately. However, once you create a schedule and make it a priority to carve out some hours of your week to attend to your hobbies, you will start noticing all-round growth of your personality. It would propel you to treat time as a limited resource and understand the importance of effective time management.

Next time you evaluate how your week went, you may realize that you completely forgot to call your old friend whom you had thought of while preparing the sheet, or perhaps you completely ignored looking into a particular policy of your business you had aimed to review. Evaluating one's schedule at the end of the week is a great method of self-introspection. No one forced you to write your weekly goals. You wrote them yourself and you were perhaps really motivated when making the schedule.

When you realize at the end of the week that you hardly accomplished much, it naturally prompts reflection on how you are spending your time. Over a few months, you will subconsciously start building good time management patterns and realize which activities are actually a priority for you.

I have personally seen the positive effects of scheduling in my own life. From spending several hours a day aimlessly daydreaming, I am now efficiently completing projects by consistently investing my efforts within a set time frame. An example of how scheduling helped me is through the project of establishing 'OKRs' in my organization. I had read a book called *Measure What Matters* by John Doer, where I came across the fantastic concept of replacing 'key responsibility areas (KRAs)' with 'objectives and key results (OKRs)'. I envisioned the benefits this model would have in my family business and how this model would bring accountability to the forefront.

I wanted to implement this project, but it felt daunting to set OKRs for different departments. Without getting into the intricate details of OKRs, as that is not the purpose of this book, what I want to share is that I simply kept delaying this project with an excuse that I could not find time. The issue was not the lack of time but a lack of a proper schedule. By creating a schedule and putting this project in my weekly activities list, I managed to finally get started. After sitting with members from each department and doing my own research, I managed to set OKRs for six departments in my organization. This project took 45 days to complete, and now we have a detailed process flow of measuring key business-generation activities on a weekly basis. It was only possible to complete this project while working on the core business activities through the power of scheduling.

Of course, I do acknowledge that I have a great team, excellent resources and a strong support system behind me, which made it possible to take out time for the OKR project. However, I perhaps always had those things, but I never really valued them. I was so busy solving day-to-day problems that I never really got the time to evaluate our mission statement and focus on high-leverage activities. Now, with a weekly schedule, I can assess my activities and plan ahead for things that truly lead to holistic growth.

Although the meaning of holistic growth differs for each of us, we can all agree that our aim is to become well-rounded individuals. But how much time are we dedicating to prioritizing activities that may lead to our holistic growth? Do we even know how we plan to get there, or are we simply grinding day after day, hoping to stumble on this illusive concept of holistic growth?

See, scheduling your time is a choice. It is probably an uncomfortable choice in the beginning because it requires a lot of self-introspection. I gave an example earlier—how reviewing our weekly activity at the end of the week can highlight things we missed—like calling an old friend. Just writing that activity at the start of the week could be uncomfortable because we would realize that perhaps we had not spoken to that close friend in six months. On the other hand, if we keep living life in hustle mode without any scheduling, these thoughts never arise because we are not giving ourselves the opportunity to pause and reflect. We may be living with the satisfaction that we are working as hard as possible, but after a few years we will look back at lost time and realize there were so many fulfilling activities we completely ignored.

The takeaway is clear: prioritize your activities, realize that you cannot do each and every thing you want, respect time as a limited resource, and finally, begin the art of scheduling. Doing so will make your professional life productive while allowing you to live a wholesome life with friends and family.

To my reader: When was the last time you met a close friend from your school or college, or explored a new hobby? Do you feel you are unable to find time to do things outside of your core business? I would encourage you to begin with creating a weekly planner for yourself. Remember to include not just your business-related activities but your personal and social goals as well. Ask yourself, 'Am I ready to allocate time to things that are not really urgent in my life but are indeed important in my long-term development?' Of course, to prioritize an activity, you will have to learn to say no to things as well. That is what I am going to talk about in the next chapter.

12

Nurture the Power to Say 'No'

Introspect and understand what you really want in your life.

Since we were kids, it was ingrained in us that a good student is someone who is punctual in submitting homework, sincere in class, respectful towards elders, proactive in keeping the room clean and following the advice of teachers. We were also told to avoid bad habits such as not brushing our teeth, not biting our nails, not coming late to class, etc. The above habits are universally considered as 'good' or 'bad' and it is easy to identify them.

As we grew older and went to college, the bad habits came to include smoking, drinking, not getting enough sleep, and so on. Irrespective of whether someone drinks or smokes, they will never tell you it is a good habit. We all recognize what a universally accepted bad habit is, and we can then make a choice whether we still want to do it or not.

This chapter is not about passing a judgement if you do drink or smoke. Rather, it is about moving beyond the easily identifiable bad habits to examine the things we regularly say 'yes' to that may be quietly hindering our growth in the long run.

As a young entrant in the family business, the initial stages can feel overwhelming as you get up to speed with workplace dynamics. Employees may look up to you for guidance, although you don't really have much idea about your business yet. While you have a general understanding about what your company does, you are still settling in.

You are aware that employees approach you for guidance largely because of the expectations they have based on your status as a next-generation entrant in the family business. Senior family members will also regularly brief you on their perceptions of the company and suggest that you take responsibility for certain areas. As youngsters, we have been taught to follow instructions well, but we are no longer teenagers in a rebellious phase. We are now adults stepping into our family businesses, often unsure of where to begin.

Your friends, who you are hanging out with, are perhaps also business owners. Some have been there longer than you, and some, like you, are just entering the family business. When you share your experiences with each other, it is tempting to have a sense of comfort by agreeing on certain points such as:

- 'Family business comes with a lot of pressure because we are directly dealing with our relatives.'
- 'Everyone thinks it's easy working in the family business, but no one really appreciates what we, as a young entrant, go through.'
- 'Our employees don't really care about the business.'
- 'I need to go on a vacation to clear my mind because the family business environment is too stressful.'

Now look, you have to decide whether you are in the family business to transform the company or simply live a comfortable life where you are only concerned with maintaining the business with a modest, incremental growth. When you hang out with your business friends, I would suggest taking a moment to reflect whether most of your conversations revolve around the above points.

It is natural—and healthy—to discuss challenges and vent your feelings at times. However, be aware of whether your circle is making you think and introspect, or if it has become an echo chamber where gossip and complaints dominate the discussion. I do acknowledge that many people join the family business because they have no other choice. You might be one of them. But the difference is that you *do* have a choice now.

Coming back to the earlier example, we are all aware that smoking is bad. In fact, if you ask most people why they started smoking, they would say that it's because all their friends would smoke too. This small example has a deep meaning behind it. Our social group and our friend circle define us but we can still maintain boundaries if we showcase assertiveness. I know of a lot of people who left a particular group of friends because they were the only non-smoker in that group, or who were still a part of all group activities but firmly said 'no' when it came to that one activity they didn't want to participate in. Similarly, before becoming a part of a new group of friends, it is important for you to first think about what you really want. If we don't know who we are and what we desire from life, we will keep going with the flow in the hopes of fitting in. Once we have done the work on ourselves and have a basic understanding of what our goals are, we start recognizing whether we want to say 'yes' to certain things.

Let us take a work-related example. You have had an unpleasant moment in your family business. You lost your temper and behaved rudely with a senior employee. You don't feel good about it and find yourself wondering how you lost control over your emotions. You then meet a group of friends and share this incident with them, and they dismiss it is as being a normal part of working in a business. Now, you were initially unhappy with your actions, but their casual acceptance makes you feel it was no big deal. So, when you lose your temper for the second time, you justify it as simply being a normal part of working in a business. Soon, this behaviour is normalized in your mind even though you were uncomfortable with it the first time it took place.

In the long run, you risk becoming like any other entitled young family business owner who simply loses their cool and berates employees. The core issue was not that you have a tendency to lose your temper. We all can work on controlling our emotions once we become aware of the negative impact it has on the people around us. The real issue was that your friend circle justified your behaviour even though you were unsure, and you quickly agreed with their assessment. In other words, you let yourself off the hook.

Learning to say 'no' does not mean you don't listen to the opinions of others. It means hearing them out but instead of simply accepting it as the norm, you pause to assess whether they are aligned with your own beliefs. I have seen many of my peers who were fundamentally against a particular way of life only months earlier but ended up changing their way of thinking. Upon discussions, I realized that this change did not come from introspecting whether the new way of life had a positive impact on their lives, but rather from the fear of saying 'no' and losing that particular circle of friends.

There could be many uncomfortable emotions we deal with when it comes to our business, relationships, mental health, physical appearance, etc. When we learn to say 'no' to normalizing these uncomfortable feelings, we say 'yes' to exploring our emotions more deeply and asking ourselves those tough questions to get a better understanding of our character. Remember that when you say 'no' to something, you are saying 'yes' to something else.

If you feel all this is nice to hear but tough to implement, well I agree with you. It is indeed not easy to nurture the ability to say 'no' as agreeableness is a highly respected trait in our society, especially with our seniors. Moreover, once you say refuse to participate in a certain activity or a certain proposal, you are taking ownership and responsibility. It is easier to be the sixth person to agree to a plan if the other five have already given their approval.

At the same time, you don't want to be saying 'no' just for the sake of it or to be different. The only way you can say 'no' with conviction is when you are aware of what you really want, you are ready to take responsibility in case your way does not work and your reason for saying 'no' is not just for grabbing attention.

If you are convinced that you want to invest your time and efforts to transform the family business, you must learn to say 'no' to comfort and 'yes' to exploration. I am not telling you to make any dramatic changes in your life or give up any existing habits. What may work for me may or may not work for you. Nurturing something is not about instant results; it's a process that leads to long-term returns.

Similarly, to nurture the ability to say 'no' is to become more aware of the environment around you. It is to resist saying 'yes' to things at face value without realizing the long-term impact it might have on your development. As a young entrant in my family business, I have seen my business circle change over the past few years. During the initial period, while I was getting to know about my business, I had a particular set of friends I needed at the time. They helped me de-stress and relax whenever work became too overwhelming. As mentioned earlier in my book, I was not sure at that stage how much time I would like to invest in my family business, and with that approach, I hung out with a lot of people with similar thoughts. As I became more invested in the family business, I realized that this was an area that I was now passionate about. But this thought did not resonate much with most people in my circle.

While I unfortunately did not relate with their views anymore, I did not want to lose my circle of friends, and so I continued meeting them despite not being mentally present during the discussions. As time passed and I became more aware, I realized that the reason I hang out with my old group is not because I feel it is rude to move away from a circle of friends just because our views no longer match, but because I am concerned that I won't be able to find a new circle who would relate to my existing thought process. I worked upon this feeling for a few weeks and gradually, I began making active efforts to find people who were passionate about their businesses too.

I was on the lookout for youngsters who were ready to invest a lot of time in transforming their business culture. In a year or two, my circle had completely transformed. While I am still in touch with my initial group, I don't spend a lot of time with them anymore. It's not like there were any issues with my initial group of friends, and they are a lovely bunch of people; but it's just that our priorities had changed over time. If I had not nurtured the ability to say 'no', I would be hanging out with a group of very nice people who were not too passionate about their business, whereas I was getting really involved in transforming my business. By reflecting and taking time to say 'yes' to a change, I met more people, and that led to new conversations, new ideas, new points for explorations and new experiences.

It takes courage to self-reflect and explore those uncomfortable feelings. In the modern world of YouTube Shorts and Insta Reels, we are constantly seeking quick fixes for everything. When I started writing this book, I had a template on the points I thought I would like to cover. However, I noticed that after writing consistently for a while, I started slacking off and procrastinating. After a few weeks of no writing, I began wondering why this was happening. Quickly, I would brush the feeling aside by justifying that I had been quite busy with personal, professional and social engagements.

Two months later, I decided to take a deeper look. After some honest introspection, I admitted that I had simply been saying 'yes' to a lot of distractions without realizing the impact it was having on the very project I cared deeply about—this book. This uncomfortable confrontation helped me get back and continue with my writing from this chapter onwards.

I firmly believe there is no magic formula or no motivational speech that can keep you going consistently forever. The one habit that will enable you to get back on track in life is 'self-awareness'. Becoming more aware of your goals, your desires, your roadmap that you have set for yourself enables you to review your habits and say 'no' to everything that no longer fits in your life goals. As emphasized before, it is indeed tough and requires a lot of conviction.

To my reader: I would encourage you to write down three activities you are doing regularly but you no longer feel they add positive impact in your life. Could you devise a strategy to phase out these activities? Making a list of three new activities you feel will add value to your life will assist in this transition. Letting go of things you have been doing for a long time is not easy, but it is necessary for your sustained growth. The one thing that makes it a little easier to nurture the power of saying 'no' is having a strong conviction that good things will happen to you. Does this sound impractical? How can you just know that good things will happen to you? Well, I will talk about this in the next chapter.

13

Realize That Good Things Will Happen to You

Identify the positive aura in your life.

You may be a religious person, or you may know someone who is. Many of us offer prayers on a regular basis, eat certain types of food during religious occasions and we are convinced that there is a God above looking after us. Some of us are not sure of God's existence but we believe there is a higher power at work whom we perhaps refer to as the 'Universe'. Some of us do not believe in God or in Universe and are indifferent to the concept of a higher power. No matter which category you belong to, if an unfavourable incident has happened in your life, you have probably asked the question, 'Why me?'

Yes, this is a question we often ask ourselves when something unfortunate happens in our lives. But are we taking out the time to acknowledge how many special things have fallen in our laps? Today, there are many youngsters who anxiously wait to find out the kind of job they would secure after graduating. There are youngsters who are convinced they can add a lot more value in their company, but as entry level employees, they are not given the authority to take decisions. Then there are those who have seen their family business thrive when they were kids but also witnessed the business close down by the time they were entering college. If you could not relate to what I just mentioned, you should take a moment right now to acknowledge the privileged life you have and practise gratitude.

You are receiving the golden opportunity to enter a family business and make a difference from day one. The stars have somehow conspired to grant you this opportunity instead of giving it to a billion others. Now, you have the privilege to make use of this opportunity gifted to you, for which you have not really done anything. Yes, you will indeed be working hard to take your business to greater heights, but the chance to walk into an established business as an owner from day one is a massive stroke of luck. It is equally important now to accept this stroke of luck gracefully and acknowledge that good things have happened to you, and that they will continue to take place in your life.

Yes, I am asking you to *realize* that good things will happen to you. It is not something you have to assume. Realization is defined as 'coming to understand something clearly and distinctly.' Look back at your life and think of certain events that have taken place over which you had no control. For example, the life you have lived due to the place you were born in, the best friend you made in school despite not having any choice in the school-selection process, the surprise birthday party your loved ones planned for you where you ended up having a wonderful time, the precious item you had misplaced a long time ago, which you one day found randomly when cleaning your room, a restaurant you enter where the host orders an item that does not seem appealing, but you end up trying it and fall in love with it. The list is endless, but the point is to take a few deep breaths and reflect on certain good things that have happened in your life during the past few years and realizing that perhaps it is not just a coincidence. That, in fact, it is the higher powers being friendly to you.

Having such a realization gives you an immense sense of conviction. There is no way to prove what I am saying is true but what is required here is to reflect and realize how many times we have brushed away our good fortunes and replayed certain unfavourable occasions over and over again.

When you join the family business, you are inevitably under pressure from expectations. Everyone around you is convinced that you are the one who must take the business to greater heights. At times things may get overwhelming. It becomes tough to take new decisions and initiatives if you constantly think about what may go wrong and what if you make a fool of yourself. On such occasions, it is crucial that you self-reflect and realize that good things are going to happen to you. When you take up new initiatives with sincerity and conviction, it will make a positive impact on you and your surroundings.

Let me give an example. When I joined my family business in 2014 after completing my graduation from New Zealand, I wanted to bring professionalism to our traditional office events. Across the world, 1 May is celebrated as International Workers' Day. In 2012, my father had started an initiative to celebrate this day in the industrial city of Durgapur, West Bengal, as 'International Workers' Day and Drivers' Day', because as a logistics company, we wanted to pay our respects to truck drivers who are an integral part of the workforce. At that time, I was in university, and I would hear about my father and other senior family members' efforts to execute this event.

Upon returning to India, I witnessed our Drivers' Day celebrations for the first time in 2015. I realized that although this day was celebrated with a lot of pride and good intentions, there was a feeling of dissatisfaction in my father. It was because the drivers would often remark that the company celebrates them for one day but then ignores them for the rest of the year. Many senior employees would resign themselves to the fact that, after all, we cannot expect anything more from truck drivers, and they must be grateful for the initiatives the company takes for them. However, I thought differently.

I completely acknowledged the efforts and the positive thought process behind my father's vision for celebrating 1 May as not just Workers' Day but also as Drivers' Day. However, the issue was that although the senior managers were behind his vision for celebrating the day, they did not really communicate or interact with drivers on other days, and this led to resentment amongst the truck drivers. After understanding this issue, I set out to do something that did not exist in the Indian software space at the time—humanizing truck drivers through a dedicated software platform. Each driver in our company was registered and given a complete online profile, including a driver code, blood group, home address, list of family members, emergency contact numbers, and other essential details. We further created a portal where every single leave taken by the drivers was recorded and an HR team was created to follow up with truck drivers to ensure they returned to duty on time. It is a prevalent issue across India that most truck drivers do not return to the same company after going on a leave, and I wanted to change this behaviour.

By celebrating the human element of our truck drivers, we started building rapport through structured interactions and data analysis. Every single interaction was recorded in our portal so that even if a new employee was speaking with the truck driver, they had all the necessary information to have an effective communication with them instead of just checking a box.

Did the attitude of our drivers change immediately? No. In fact, it took us three years (from 2016 to 2019) to document the data of over 100 truck drivers and create their profiles, along with a history of the trucks driven by them, total leaves taken since joining, any relatives working in our organization and any other drivers referred by them.

Further, I had observed that in case any road accidents took place, it was the driver who was always blamed and penalized. After discussing with my father, we came up with a new initiative—there would be a video interaction of the driver in presence of two senior employees and two drivers, so we could get an unbiased view of the incident instead of simply blaming the truck driver. Our initiatives were recognized over time by not just our drivers, but by *EXIM India*, India's leading shipping and logistics newspaper. We were honoured with a national award for 'Best Practices in Driver Management' in 2020. Today, at a time when the world is grappling with a shortage of truck drivers, our company maintains 95 per cent fleet utilization at all times, supported by a team of drivers who trust the organization.

Collaborating with a software company to create a comprehensive driver software, going through the pains of following up with truck drivers to collect data, and all this while ignoring the noise around us that focusing on transforming driver behaviour is a waste of time—this mindset was only possible because we had a strong conviction that goods things will happen to our company and that our truck driver satisfaction would increase if we persisted with an open mind to hear feedback. Starting this one initiative with a positive intent led to the creation of numerous events in the future that boosted our driver management practice and has helped us become a 'Great Place to Work'-certified organization with a fleet of 150 plus trucks.

Realizing and strongly believing that good things will happen to us, is a huge stimulant for getting things started. After all, our subconscious is an extremely powerful tool. Whenever we have doubts about starting an initiative, our subconscious senses this and gives us hundreds of 'logical' excuses such as:

- I am not ready yet.
- I have a big project coming up in 2–3 months, so let me first work on that before starting this initiative.
- I just don't have time to spend on developmental works; first let me get more clients and increase my profits, then I will worry about anything else.
- There is no guarantee this initiative will work, I would rather stick to a tried-and-tested formula.
- I don't think people will accept this initiative. Let me re-evaluate this next year.

I am sure you could relate to at least two of the above points when it comes to starting a new initiative. All these excuses boil down to the simple emotion that we are not fully convinced good things will happen to us. We are so suspicious of the Universe and the people around us that we feel it is safer to go with the flow. During times when such thoughts come in our heads, it is important to reflect on the simple exercises mentioned earlier in the chapter. Think of all those moments when goods things happened to you without making any effort, and what if instead of labelling those events as lucky, we actually started believing that the Universe is with us. In my experience, if we take one intentional step to start a new initiative and we are honest in our efforts, then the Universe will do everything in its power to make our vision a reality.

You may be convinced that there are people who are just waiting for you to make a mistake or to fail in your role as the new entrant in the family business. There is a strong probability that they have never told you this on your face, but you sense this based on their behaviour. Dwelling on these feelings hinders your ability to take new initiatives and to fully immerse yourself in the business.

My message is that you are not going to gain anything by obsessing over such thoughts. Growth takes place when you start exploring your core competencies and understanding how you can add value to the business through your talents. If you indeed have a tendency to ponder over what others are feeling about you, then why not focus on the ones who want you to succeed. Speak with them, share your inputs and the ideas you have. Do this with a strong realization that goods things are going to happen based on the initiatives you are planning. That energy will flow through them, and you may get constructive suggestions too.

With the added confidence, you can perhaps start approaching the people whom you sense want you to fail. What if they start realizing your interest in making an impact and it creates a chain reaction where you start getting constructive feedback from them as well? This might be considered wishful thinking, but the truth is we are the most important person in our lives, not in the lives of others. Those assumptions we have of certain people not liking us may or may not be true, but what is certain is that no one thinks about us as much as we think they do. Let me repeat this:

No one thinks about us as much as we think they do.

It simply means that we often let certain people's thoughts and opinions live in our head, and we constantly feed these thoughts to give them more power. Unless someone comes up to you and tells you that they do not like certain things you are doing or certain ideas you are planning to implement, do not assume.

In this chapter, my message is clear. Focus on the things that will make you grow. Instead of having assumptions, know one thing—that good things will happen to you.

To my reader: Can you identify five good things that happened in your life this past year that made you feel lucky? Spend some time and introspect. If you are finding it tough to identify these five things, dig deeper and think of something that may appear to be small but still made you feel happy during that moment. Acknowledging the good things that come your way in the journey of life will help you inculcate gratitude for things most of us take for granted.

This realization will make you look at the world differently and enable you to identify opportunities that are right in front of you but you have been ignoring. It will also make you understand that there is a beautiful world out there in which you can create a lasting impact. The realization will make you question a concept which is frequently shared as the 'truth' in our society—it's called 'give and take'. Over the years, you will shun this concept and embrace a more transformational idea—that of 'give and receive'. I will share about this concept in the next chapter.

14

Imbibe the Concept of 'Give and Receive'

Let go of preconceived notions and approach your business with a fresh mindset.

The transactional values of the material world are taught to us since our childhood. By the time we reach our late teens, the concept of 'give and take' has already taken deep root. As a child growing up, it was common to hear phrases like: 'There are no free lunches,' 'Everything comes at a cost,' 'Never do anything for free,' and a phrase that was considered a little kinder, 'First give and then take.'

All these sayings stem from the same belief—that only after putting in effort or offering something can we expect to take what we want. In fact, this policy of 'give and take' is deeply embedded in the family business world. We are taught to pay respect to our seniors to get their approval, make quick decisions to take advantage of market conditions and be friends with the right people to avail indirect benefits.

I personally found it really tough to make meaningful connections with people in the professional world with this concept of 'give and take'. When a relationship is judged based on what we get in comparison with what we give, it becomes almost impossible to develop empathy, compassion and mutual respect.

We often hear people in our circle discuss how they gave so many opportunities to a particular person, but that person left their family business for a better offer in another company; and there is now a feeling of bitterness towards the individual. This is because the person who gave the opportunities did so with the expectation that they would get back favourable returns from their actions. Such relationships often, if not always, end up with one winner and one loser. The moment we are doing something with an expectation of getting something better out of it, is when we lose the human element of a relationship.

Take a deep breath and look back at your professional relationships. If you are working with a colleague or an employee or a business partner, do you sometimes wonder who is benefitting more from that relationship? It's okay; this is nothing to be concerned about because society has trained us in a manner where we are conditioned to desire the best personal outcome from each professional relationship. I have met people who have preached that each individual has an ulterior motive behind any act of kindness or appreciation. I am not debating whether they are right or wrong, I am simply stating that this is not a philosophy that has been useful for my growth.

To create sustained growth and build holistic relationships, I believe in a different concept: 'give and receive'. Now this might come as a downer for you because you may wonder: What is the difference between 'give and take' and 'give and receive'? It sounds like the same thing.

Well, let us explore this.

The textbook definition of 'take' as per Merriam-Webster is:

> to get into one's hands or into one's possession, power, or control, such as:
>
> a. to seize or capture physically
> b. to get possession of (fish or game) by killing or capturing
> c. (1) to move against (an opponent's piece, as in chess) and remove from play
>   (2) to win in a card game
> d. to acquire by eminent domain…

As you can see, some of the words and phrases associated with describing the word 'take' are 'power', 'control', 'seize', 'capturing', 'killing'; and these set an aggressive and violent tone to the word 'take'.

Now, compare this to the word 'receive', which is defined in Merriam-Webster as:

> 1. to come into possession of
> 2. (a) to act as a receptacle or container for
>   (b) to assimilate through the mind or senses
> 3. (a) to permit to enter
>   (b) welcome, greet…

The word 'receive' displays a kinder undertone with phrases and terms such as 'act as a receptacle', 'assimilate', 'permit', 'welcome', and 'greet'. Such words and phrases can be considered friendly.

Yes, words are a powerful tool, and by replacing the word 'take' with the word 'receive', we can change our entire outlook towards our professional as well as our personal relationships.

It is indeed liberating to *give* without *taking* something in return. In fact, the concept of 'giving and receiving' provides a sense of security—that you are definitely going to receive what you want once you offer your expertise, support or efforts to something or someone. By eliminating the transactional undertone from the relationship, we can transform ourselves and our surroundings.

During the past few years, I have come across people who truly believe in the concept of 'giving' without expectations of 'taking' something in return. These people are calm, secure and have a wonderful outlook towards life. They know that their honest deeds are sufficient to pave the way for a bright and prosperous life. They are putting in their efforts sincerely without any fear of the outcome because somewhere their mind is certain that they will always receive the result they seek.

In a family business scenario, I have applied this philosophy of 'give and receive' at work, and it has worked wonders for me and my organization. The concept of 'giving' without the expectation of 'taking' something can be easily implemented with our employees.

In my book, I have already discussed about the importance of hiring a candidate in a systematic manner through a robust hiring process. Once we hire an employee, we must give them opportunities to apply their skills and develop their potential. Here, several business owners remain on the fence when it comes to upskilling employees because they feel that the employee may leave the company, and their cost of training would go waste. Well, I won't deny that it is always disappointing to lose good talent, especially once they have become a dependable asset in daily operations. However, imbibing the attitude of 'give and receive' can completely change your outlook towards such a scenario.

On a personal level, I have trained several employees who were freshers when they joined the company. I firmly believed in giving them as many opportunities as possible so that they could grow and in turn add value to the organization. As someone who has received the privilege of joining a family business where one can take key decisions from an early stage of career, I wanted to give opportunities to newcomers to apply their skillset and take decisions. This accelerated the rate of growth of our organization and made youngsters feel valued. The newcomers felt grateful that, unlike what they would hear from their friends in other companies who were instructed to simply follow instructions, they had the opportunity to apply their minds and take calculated risks. Of course, there was supervision involved, and not all their ideas were accepted, yet the important part was that the employees felt 'heard', and this is something which meant a lot to them. Did all newcomers stay in our organization? Of course not! But there are two ways to look at this scenario:

1 Despite giving opportunities to newcomers, they still left for other opportunities, and hence it was a waste of time giving them so much freedom.	2 Although the newcomers eventually left, they contributed immensely during their time at the organization, and this led to an improvement in workplace culture.

As stated earlier, neither of the two scenarios are right or wrong. It simply depends on the kind of philosophy you wish to adopt.

Yes, it is completely understandable to feel bitter if you gave opportunities to your employees for growth and they ended up leaving your organization for other lucrative options. During such times, it is important to realize that we no longer live in a time where employees are joining your company for survival. People today want to work at a job where they have a purpose. The sense of belongingness and self-worth is crucial to workplace satisfaction. If we, as business owners, can decide to quit a new business project and move on to another, why can't employees think of quitting a job and moving on to another opportunity that may be better in their view.

The second scenario is nothing more than a mindset shift. When we approach a situation with the attitude of giving and receiving, we tend to value our time in a better manner. Instead of worrying about the future—which is uncertain anyway—we make sure we make the most of the time we have each day. If we feel an employee has potential, we look towards guiding them and enabling them to fulfil their potential.

By managing a workplace with this mindset, we realize that, in the long run, it is the organization that is the eventual winner. It is always preferable to have a welcoming work environment where smart and talented individuals work sincerely for a few years or perhaps even months, rather than an autocratic work environment where employees are scared to speak up and are only working due to a need for survival instead of aspirations for growth.

The concept of 'give and receive' is equally applicable to our vendors and clients. It is interesting to observe negotiations where both parties are sitting at the table with low trust. In such cases, the concept of 'give and take' dominates, and neither party is happy after the negotiation is complete. The sense of insecurity looms large as both parties are fearful that they were worse off after the deal.

In contrast, imagine a scenario where you meet your client with a sincere intention to add value to their business with your product or service. You are approaching the negotiation with your best intentions to solve the client's problems, and you have a sense of security that you will receive your desired result from the discussion. Suddenly, the 'negotiation' changes to 'fruitful discussion'. You are still making the same preparations, doing your homework, analysing data and presenting your proposal—but now, your mindset is different. You are confident that the client will understand your requirements because you are guided by a sincere desire to improve their operations.

This mindset is not going to be achieved in a day. But with time and with steady steps, you will realize how your life and your family business start transforming once you start *giving* with a profound certainty that you will *receive* the desired outcome, without the need to *take* something from the other party.

Take the case of dealing with vendors. From my observations of various business owners, I find it interesting that many complain about their clients not understanding their problems, yet they often display the same behaviour when dealing with their vendors. We need to come out of the mindset that someone else must change first before we make the change. Instead, we must actively work towards imbibing a philosophy of treating our vendors the way we would like our clients to treat us.

This does not translate to giving in to any unreasonable demands our vendors put on us or not working towards getting the best prices for our company. It simply means that we first approach interactions with our vendors from a sense of respect. We understand the value which a good vendor adds to the organization and we realize that we have to *give* a fair deal to our vendor to *receive* our desired service. Having disgruntled vendors can lead to negative PR (public relations). Companies mention lofty stories about their policies and their ethical standards, but it is interactions with vendors that help us gauge the true work culture of any organization. If your vendor is treated well, they make sure to give positive feedback about your company to the market. This is invaluable for your company's reputation.

I cannot emphasize enough: the principle 'give and receive' cannot be applied on a case-to-case basis. We cannot expect to simply imbibe this attitude with our clients while treating our vendors and employees with a transactional 'give and take' mindset. For a healthy workplace culture to develop—and for your stakeholders to truly believe that the family business is evolving from an environment where employees were expected merely to follow instructions to a modern, family-run organization where employees are treated as team members and customers no longer rely simply on family members for solutions—it is imperative that there is trust amongst the stakeholders.

Trust will grow when you, as the next generation of your family business, begin to take those first steps to truly create an environment where the members around you start realizing your intentions. Will there be employees, vendors or clients who will take undue advantage of this philosophy? Perhaps. However, the gains will far outweigh the shortcomings. My company stands as a shining example of this.

During COVID-19 lockdown, we heard countless stories of pay cuts and layoffs. Several Indian companies followed suit. They reduced salaries because operation had halted during the quarantine phase in the initial months. Our company, too, faced challenges. And although we are in the logistics sector, which is an essential service, there were various people who were stuck at home and could not join work.

At this juncture, we could have done what most other companies did—cut pay because employees were unable to contribute to business operations. But we did not do this because we realized that we would not be able to create an atmosphere of trust if we did not go that that extra mile to ensure the financial security of our workforce during a pandemic. When our employees received their full salary, they started to believe that the company genuinely valued their well-being and security during uncertain times.

The response was remarkable. Employees expressed heartfelt gratitude and made sincere efforts to contribute to the company's growth. Had we opted to cut pay like most companies, we would have lost out on our workplace culture, which takes years to rebuild. This experience was transformational—an enlightenment that showed us how *giving* with the assurance that we will *receive* the fruits of our efforts leads to abundance: an abundance of gratitude, prosperity and success.

There are countless examples where 'give and receive' has worked wonders. It's important to continue giving with the assurance that the dots will connect in the future. With this mindset, we won't need to worry about the results, because the process will take precedence. Results will follow once we have processes in place and when we continue living with this transformational mindset.

To my reader: Can you think of a scenario in your life where you were unsatisfied with what you got back after all the efforts you put in? It could be related to dealing with a client, a family member, a friend, or even a course you spent time on. Now, re-evaluate the same scenario, but through the lens of 'give and receive'. How might you rewrite this story in your head to recognize what you actually gained from your efforts—benefits you may not have noticed before? Once we begin adopting the mindset of 'give and receive', we open ourselves to transformation through attracting abundance in our lives. I will talk about the concept of attracting abundance in the next chapter.

15

Dissociate from Fear-Based Thinking to Attract Abundance

Create positive impact by overcoming your fear of failure.

'Based on my study of the company's balance sheet and financial records of the past three years, I want to implement a new policy in my family business. But let me analyse the data for a few more months before going ahead.'

'I have been observing this particular employee's behaviour towards others as well as their approach towards office work, and it is very negative. But we are not ready to run our operations smoothly without this employee. So let me observe them for a few more months before taking any steps.'

'I want to pursue my hobby of playing sports, but I am not ready to wake up in the morning yet.'

'Based on our product life-cycle analysis, I am confident that our products don't match the sustainability and environment norms of the present day, but I am not ready to change a tried and tested formula.'

Do any of the above phrases seem relatable? Chances are that they do. We often have intuitions, and then we analyse them to uncover whether they are well-founded. It is important to not just act based on our whims and fancies. Yes, understanding the consequences of our actions is important, and I have always admired family-run businesses that think through their actions before implementing them. I am not advising you, as the youngster in your family business, to jump into decision-making mode simply based on your intuitions. But what I intend to communicate through this chapter is that once we analyse our intuitions and find that they are well-founded, there is only one reason to not act. It is the fear of failure.

As youngsters in the family business, we are entering a domain where we have the opportunity to take ownership from day one. Although this is exhilarating but it also has the drawback of facing the consequences of all our decisions, no matter how big or small they are. It may appear daunting to take actions in this scenario because the buck stops with you. Yes, your senior family members in the management will be guiding you and you will need to convince them before you implement a new business strategy—but eventually it is you who will take ownership of the results of those decisions.

During such scenarios, we often get stuck in the 'thinking trap'. This is a comfortable zone where we observe our work environment, analyse the data at our disposal, arrive at a conclusion and devise a plan of action. However, we never take intentional steps to execute our plan as we believe that our organization is not ready yet. We wait for the environment to be 'perfect' before we may implement our plans, and as a result, precious time passes by.

The environment is never going to be perfect. But

we keep waiting and blaming external factors for not implementing our strategies. Whereas the biggest reason holding us back is our internalized fear of failure. It is common while growing up to receive advice from our elders that one should not take unnecessary risks or that one should be fully prepared before sitting for an exam. While this is a great piece of advice, perhaps we started interpreting it the wrong way as we grew older. Yes, it is true that we should not take unnecessary risks, but we must be careful to not trick our mind into believing something to be an unnecessary risk, just because we are too scared to start.

Let us take the first sentence mentioned earlier as an example:

'Based on my study of the company's balance sheet and financial records of the past three years, I want to implement a new policy in my family business. But let me analyse the data for a few more months before going ahead.'

In this case, we have spent a considerable amount of time researching before deciding to implement a new policy in the family business. Yet, we want to spend more time analysing the data because our fear of failure is tricking us into believing that we may be taking an unnecessary risk by coming up with a new policy. Our logical brain has done its calculations and data analysis, and it has passed on the message that we need to implement something, but our lizard brain convinces us that we should stall for some more time.

The 'lizard brain' is a term to describe that primitive, risk-averse part of our brain that constantly reminds us of potential dangers ahead. In this case, what would actually have been a calculated step based on our logical analysis is being perceived as an unnecessary risk by our lizard brain.

The first step is to become aware of this and realize that feeling scared is normal. The next step could be to have a discussion with our family members and senior managers to involve them in the analysis. The next step could also be to create a first draft of the policy and plan a trial with a smaller group. By doing so, you step out of your comfort zone and embrace a motto that has helped me grow in my career: 'It is tough as well as scary, and I am going to do it anyway.'

This mindset frees us from the shackles of reactive, backfoot management and propels us towards proactive leadership. Will this mindset develop in one day? No. Will it take several years to nurture this mindset? No. As mentioned above, I would like to re-emphasize that the first step is acknowledging the fear and realizing that it is okay to be scared. The moment we become aware of our internal fears that are stopping us from taking action, we can start working on them. Just like muscles are developed by showing up at the gym consistently, our ability to take initiative strengthens gradually. The initial moves may be small but meaningful, and once we start recognizing the ripple effect of our proactiveness, we never look back.

One common concern I often hear from youngsters in family businesses is their fear of starting a new initiative because a similar initiative failed miserably in their friend's organization. It is important to note that each organization has its own dynamic, history, industry-specific challenges, employer–employee relations, competitive advantages and limitations. It may well be true that a comparable initiative did not succeed elsewhere, but it is oversimplified thinking to assume that the initiative was executed in the exact same manner as we have planned, or that the other organization did the exact same data analysis before starting their initiative.

When I further probe into this reluctance to begin something new, I understand that the real issue is indeed the fear of failure. We are expecting every single person in our extended circle to approve our ideas before we begin. If some of them do not give their approval or if some of them share examples of how similar initiatives failed in other known organizations, we start getting anxious. Negative self-talk takes over: *What if it fails? What if people say, 'See, I told you so.'*

To avoid this scenario, which may or not may not happen in the future, we end up feeding into our fear-based thinking. Challenges are inevitable when a new initiative is taken up, and many of these challenges will only come to the surface once the initiative is underway. No matter how prepared we are, it is unrealistic to assume that a new initiative will achieve its intended results without any obstacles. Therefore, once you have formulated a clear plan of action, resist the urge to conjure up challenges that are not under your control—such as whether relatives or business friends will lose their respect for you if you fail; or whether you will be discussed in a negative light for trying to change the status quo. By focusing solely on things you can control, you will be successful in identifying whether your actions, or rather your lack of action, is due to a genuine logical reason or if it is induced by fear-based thinking.

During my initial year in the business, I had a strong fear when approaching prospective clients because I felt I didn't have the expertise to answer the kind of questions they would ask me. This fear led me to make various excuses when it came to meeting potential customers. As time passed by, I started gaining more knowledge about the business, but I still felt I did not know enough to meet a prospective customer and convince them to try our company's services. I would often sit with my network of business friends and hear how they weave their way through conversations and convert new customers with their sales pitch. I would wonder how they were able to do this so easily, and through my interactions with them, I learnt of various methods they used to have a successful business meet.

One comment in particular made a deep impact on me. A friend of mine mentioned that no one can ever be ready for what the client may ask. The goal is to approach the situation with a positive mind and firmly believe that if we do not close the deal, at least we get to learn something new.

I dwelled upon this thought and realized that I need to acknowledge this fear and go and meet the new client anyway. After meeting my first potential client, I realized that the process was honestly not that scary. I had made up a story in my head to feed my fear-based thinking, which made the entire process more daunting than it actually was. Yes, I have had quite a few client meetings that did not go as per expectations, but I realized that this is part and parcel of growing as a business owner. Slowly and steadily, I began to focus on the meetings that went well and tried to repeat the things I did during those meetings. Now when I look back, I have successfully converted several potential clients to long-term customers, all because I dissociated from this fear-based approach and met new people with a positive outlook.

Awareness is the first step to overcoming a fear-based mindset. Once you have identified the self-limiting beliefs that have held you back in the past, you can begin to consciously avoid repeating them in the future. Perhaps you are planning a new initiative for your family business and feel confident it will have a positive impact. Yet, there's a part of you that worries—it would not be accepted by everyone, or worse, that you might look foolish if others disagreed with your views. That is completely fine. At least now you are aware that the feeling that is holding you back is not really based on logic but is an irrational fear driven by the risk-averse lizard brain.

With this awareness, you will be able to ask yourself certain questions that will enable you to move beyond this mindset and get things done. Guess what you will gain once you move past this fear-based mindset? You begin to attract abundance!

Abundance means a very large quantity of something. This is different from the word 'excess' which is defined as an amount that is more than acceptable, expected or reasonable.

Most of us remain stuck in the cycle of needing more things, desiring more time, expecting more lucrative outcomes, hoping for more recognition, and so on. But when we begin to take action based on the data at our disposal and the logical analysis of the information, we start moving forward. You see, not every decision will turn out to be right in the long run, but every decision will move you ahead from where you currently stand.

By breaking free from this fear-based thinking, we create space to attract abundance.

Now the question is 'how'. So let's reframe the thoughts in our head.

At the beginning of this chapter, our thought process was: *'Based on my study of the company's balance sheet and financial records of the past three years, I want to implement a new policy in my family business. But let me analyse the data for some more months before going ahead.'*

By dissociating from fear-based thinking, the same thought can be reframed as:

> Based on my study of the company's balance sheet and financial records of the past three years, I want to implement a new policy in my family business. I know that my fear of failure is tricking my mind to stall the project under the pretext of needing more data analysis. But I have already done thorough research, and I am ready to take the first step. Whatever the outcome, I know we will make progress once we begin implementing this new policy.

With this new mindset, we have acknowledged our fears because we are now aware of our risk-averse lizard brain. We have also accepted that the outcome is uncertain, for the universal truth is that the future is not guaranteed. Keeping this in mind, we are still ready to take the step and implement a new policy.

Do you realize that by taking action and by accepting ownership, you are going to impact so many more lives than you would by staying stuck in your comfort zone? People will now see you as a person who does things with the intention of making the world around you better. One decision will lead to another, which will in turn begin a series of events that starts transforming you as a person.

You begin to feel fulfilled because you are no longer procrastinating or delaying action out of fear of others' opinions. You are now ready to attract abundance into your life. Opportunities begin to appear, you find more time to implement new strategies, and positive outcomes start aligning in your favour—leading to recognition among your peers and family members.

Things start happening because you are taking action. When others are stuck in their comfort zone making excuses like you used to earlier, you are moving forward fully aware of your fears but consciously dissociating from them to move to a new world of possibilities.

A world of abundance awaits you once you start taking ownership. Instead of testing the waters with regards to your involvement in the family business, you will now be ready to dive into this wonderful and complex world with honest intentions. You will no longer wonder how you are going to make time for yourself while working in the family business, nor worry about how you can create an impact as a youngster in your company.

To my reader: I would want you to think of an initiative that you would like to implement in your family business, but you have not done it yet for the fear of failure. Now with a renewed awareness of the risk-averse lizard brain and the acknowledgement that it is okay to be scared, how would you reframe these thoughts? Once you take ownership, things begin to integrate naturally, leading to a sense of harmony. Yes, harmony in your personal and professional relations with your family is essential to achieve success in the family business. Let us discuss this in the next chapter.

16

Strive for Harmony in Your Personal and Professional Relations

Understand the root cause of issues
instead of fixing the symptoms.

As members of the Indian family business, it can often feel overwhelming being around family members all the time. I have heard first-hand stories of burnouts owing to the constant presence of family members in one's personal and professional space.

Let's take the example of an individual in the Indian corporate sector who lives with their family. Each morning, this person spends time with their family over breakfast before heading to office. In the evening, when this individual returns home, their mood may be influenced by the day at the office; but the family members are completely unaware of this. The individual may choose to narrate the day's activities to their family or avoid the discussions completely. In the case of the latter, the family's impression of the workplace develops solely through what little the individual chooses to share. The individual, on the other hand, keeps their professional and personal worlds largely separate. Their relationship with their family is based completely on their interpersonal relations with minimal influence from their professional life.

The scenario is completely different in a family-run business. Here, you interact with family members both personally at home and professionally at work. You may have always found an uncle of yours to be really helpful growing up, but you disagree with his vision for the family business. You are faced with a conundrum, because you like the uncle on a personal level, but you are having professional issues with him. This starts impacting your interactions with him at family gatherings as well.

Such situations are quite common and emotionally draining. Many of my friends in family businesses admit to falling into a self-defeating zone when they feel they cannot achieve much as their decisions are dependent on a relative's approval who is more senior in age and experience. They cite examples of how if it was a corporate setup, they would have dealt with the person with facts and data, but in a family business setup, they are cornered and hear phrases such as, 'You are too young to understand this perspective', or, 'I have raised you since you were a child; now you think you know more than me?'

Such situations lead to a loss of motivation, and I agree—it is not nice to hear such remarks. So how do we tackle them?

The first step is acknowledging that family businesses have their own unique challenges, and this is perhaps the biggest of them. The other chapters mentioned in this book have assisted you in developing a professional mindset—one that allows you to treat your organization as a corporate entity, where you have the privilege to take decisions from a very young age that can shape the future of your company and your employees. While cultivating this mindset and focusing towards a more professional work environment, how are you going to tackle the family dynamics at home?

To me, the answer lies in striving for harmony.

According to the Oxford Dictionary, the word 'harmony' is defined as: 'a state of peaceful existence and agreement'. Do note that I have mentioned that we need to *strive* for harmony instead of writing that we must achieve harmony. I am not suggesting that every family member should love each decision you make or cheer every action you take. We need to be practical—that is never going to happen. What can happen, however, is an understanding that you are making sincere efforts to advance the family business, and while there are some things that everyone may not like, there is a peaceful agreement that your efforts will be given a fair shot.

You may, for instance, be in a more senior position than a particular cousin, and when you take a particular decision which they dislike, they would consider accepting it as long as you have clearly explained your logic and reasoning. Such an understanding will contribute to a peaceful existence and help maintain relations.

The goal is to transform your family business, and that is no easy task. It is going to require you to take tough and unpopular decisions, but your willingness to strive for harmony will help you in the long run. The reason I have given a clear definition of harmony is because we often consider harmony as an extremely positive word. In reality, harmony is more neutral. It talks about peaceful existence and agreement. Yes, it is important to manage your own expectations when dealing with family-business dynamics. What you cannot afford to do is to sacrifice your business' growth just to maintain balance in your personal and professional relations.

Let me explain.

Suppose you wish to promote a particular employee in your company who is not a family member. There is a high chance you would not be able to take this decision if all the family members in your management team are not in agreement. So, let us assume that out of four family members, two are in favour but have no issue if the decision goes the other way; one is neutral and does not really care about the outcome; and one is vehemently against this move. The added complexity is that you have a strong personal relation with that one family member who is completely against this decision.

Now, if your goal is to balance your personal and professional relations, your mindset would likely be influenced by the need to maintain good relations with that family member. This will make you start evaluating the pros and cons of this decision based on how far the balance tips in favour of or against the personal relation with that family member.

You see, your decision-making lens shifts entirely. Your thought process has nothing to do with the candidate at all, anymore. It has simply become about calculating the potential 'cost' to your personal relationship. The pursuit of 'balance' in family dynamics thus becomes a constraint when it comes to taking decisions, because at the back of your mind, you are left thinking about how much of an impact a decision is taking on your equation with the family member. The actual business case takes the back seat.

Now if you look at the same scenario with a mindset to strive for *harmony* instead of *balance*, you will first manage your own expectations. You will now acknowledge that this decision is unlikely to make that family member happy, but you have already accepted that your goal is not universal approval—it is peaceful existence and agreement.

With this mindset, your focus shifts to explaining the logic behind your decision and in making sincere efforts to make your family member realize why you are doing what you are doing. You are no longer trying to please the family member with short-term gratifications to maintain a delicate equilibrium. Instead, your decision, which is purely focused on the business case, is now clearly explained to your family member with the expectation that they would understand where you are coming from. They will still not be happy with the decision, but since you are striving for harmony, the expectations regarding professional and personal relationships are much clearer now.

When we strive for harmony, our goal becomes making sincere efforts to transform our family business while maintaining a peaceful agreement with the family members involved in the organization. We focus on making sure our communication is clear, while accepting that we cannot control how others may feel about the decision. What we can control, however, is the clarity of our intentions and the professionalism with which we explain our reasoning.

In my family-run organization, I once faced a similar situation. There was a very senior employee with over two decades of experience in our company. Based on my assessment, this employee was not keen on learning new skills and was becoming complacent. Although the world was shifting rapidly towards digitalization, the employee was reluctant to learn new tools and was against adopting new systems.

After a few interactions with the person, I realized

that this employee was not against adopting new systems but was against learning digital tools from newcomers. He accepted that he needed support but found it difficult to take guidance from newcomers. Despite several discussions, sessions and handholding, I came to a realization that although this employee had great subject matter knowledge, his attitude was not conducive to the organization's growth.

The employee often withheld relevant information from his colleagues and would always present to management that the entire workload was being handled by him without much assistance from subordinates. I could notice a loss of motivation amongst the newcomers working under him as well, as they felt they did not have clear guidelines on how to complete tasks and their efforts were not being communicated to the top management through their reporting manager. Moreover, this senior employee had anger issues and would frequently have outbursts, which was detrimental to the work environment.

This employee had good relations with the family members, and I considered it my responsibility to ensure that a clear picture was presented to them. Upon hearing my arguments and the efforts taken to assist the senior employee to adjust his attitude, the elder family members had a clear discussion with the said employee. During the discussion, the employee made certain commitments to change his approach, and we agreed upon a six-month review period to evaluate progress.

When we did not see any significant changes during the six-month period, we had to take a call: Do we continue keeping an employee in the family business just because of seniority, or do we take a stand if we are indeed serious about transforming the family business? Yes, it was a tough call and there were a lot of emotions involved. Keeping the senior employee was a safer option because he was well-versed with industry norms and was efficient in his tasks. But, unfortunately, the long-term damage that was being caused by his presence could not be ignored.

We held a sit-down where we explained the vision of the company and informed him that his attitude, despite several discussions and handholding sessions, was not in sync with the way the company wanted to move forward. Did we face problems when this employee left? Definitely. But after a few years, would we consider reversing our decision of letting him go? Absolutely not!

Despite the initial few months of inconveniences, we started seeing a shift in the organization's culture. New employees realized that the company's emphasis on collaboration, cooperation and cohesiveness was backed by real action—the management was prepared to take action for non-cooperation irrespective of seniority and designation. Today, that particular department has grown leaps and bounds, and other senior employees now understand the need to adapt with the changing times.

The reason I have given a detailed explanation of this scenario from our family business is to underscore the importance of striving for harmony. When we focus merely on balancing situations, our solutions often address only the symptoms rather than the root cause of the problem. By acknowledging that there will never be a perfect balance or a flawless solution, we make sincere efforts to create a peaceful coexistence and ensure that the company steadily moves towards its vision.

So many family business owners look back and feel that had they taken that tough call a few years ago, they would not have to suffer right now. These thoughts come with a lot of baggage, because then we start blaming our surroundings and our close family members for our inactions.

That is why, it is crucial to take decisions—not with an attitude to prove we are right, but with a sincere pursuit of harmony, a genuine effort towards peaceful coexistence. Doing so will not only lead to a transformation in your family life but also bring profound improvements in your interpersonal relations with family members and your employees, whom I would like to refer to as your team members.

We hear a lot about striving for a balance in our personal and professional lives. I strongly believe that in today's interconnected world, the focus should be on striving for harmony rather than balance. In the complex family business environment, there is no end to the compromises one needs to make in playing the balancing role. In the long run, we would look back and live with regrets for the decisions we could have taken but did not just to maintain a balance in our relations with family members. Therefore, as youngsters in the family business, we must look at decision-making and our family relations with this renewed mindset to pave the way forward for transformational growth.

> **To my reader:** Is there any decision you would like to take but delaying due to the fear that it may create tension in your family environment? Think hard about this, but remember that once you start developing the mindset of striving for harmony, which is nothing but a peaceful coexistence, your decision-making would become clearer. Your focus will shift to communicating the professional reasoning behind your decisions, rather than being paralyzed by concerns about family dynamics.

Epilogue

Writing a conclusion is harder for me than writing any chapter of this book because the family business dynamics are changing each day and we learn something new all the time. The reason I wrote this book was because I strongly feel that there are so many family businesses in the world, especially those in the small and medium sector, where youngsters entering family-run companies are unable to find relatable material to read. There are several books on evolving corporate cultures, innovative management theories, digitalizing legacy operations and even conflict management in the era of AI. However, I have not come across many books focusing on the Indian family business dynamic. A book I had read and really liked on this topic was *Indian Family Business Mantras* by Peter Leach and Tatwamasi Dixit.

This book gave me an important perspective on succession planning in Indian family businesses, as well as the need to understand the dynamics between different relatives working within the enterprise. After reading this book, an idea was planted in my mind: why don't I write a book detailing my journey as a next-generation youngster entering the Indian family business.

While this book has a lot of topics that may be relatable to senior members of the family business setup and certain professionals working in a corporate setup as well, I primarily wanted to write a book for the youngsters who are entering or who have been working in the family business for a few years and want to read about the experiences of someone who is in a similar position as them.

Family businesses are complex, intimidating and, at times, frustrating. However, the joy of working in harmony with your loved ones and achieving a common goal is something beautiful. There are so many wonderful legacy family-owned companies and I take inspiration from them to transform my own family business, which is now in its third generation.

I have learnt a lot during my last 10 years working in my family business. Of my many learnings, I wanted to cover the topics I have chosen in my book because I strongly believe that family businesses are the backbone of any country. At the same time, with globalization at its peak and large-scale investors buying out companies and consolidating, it has become vital for youngsters to adopt a professional mindset within their family business context.

It is disheartening to see many industry veterans compelled to sell their family businesses because the next generation does not view the family-business set-up as prestigious enough. I have also seen the next generation joining the business but exiting after a few years because they felt it was overwhelming to take so much responsibility from such a young age. This book is for those youngsters who are looking for stories they can relate to. As next-generation members of family enterprises, we want to be heard, and we also want to listen to the stories of others who are in a similar position to ours.

Writing this book was not easy for me. This was my first attempt at writing a book, and it has taken me three years to complete this work. There were times when I got busy with my personal and professional commitments and did not write at all for months on end. Then there were times when I intentionally carved out time to review my experiences and plan the content structure of the book. There were also times when inspiration was flowing, and I would just sit in front of my laptop to write thousands of words in a single session.

To conclude, writing this book has been a wonderful learning experience. What started out as a vision to put my experiences out in public slowly transformed into a vision of making content that is relatable to the next-generation of family business owners.

There were times when I did not feel motivated enough to sit in front of my desk during my free time to work on this book, but this quote from David Bowie, the famous singer, helped me in a big way.

> Discipline doesn't mean that you make sure you have breakfast at eight o'clock in the morning and you're out of the house by half past eight. Discipline is that if you conceive something, then you decide whether or not it's worth following through. And if it's worth following through, then you follow it through to its logical conclusion and do it to the best of your ability. That's discipline.[4]

I have put in a lot of my first-hand experiences in this book, and I hope that you, my reader, has found key takeaways to introspect.

I wish you all the best in your journey of taking your family business to the next level.

---

[4]'David Bowie | Discipline | 27 November 1975', YouTube, https://tinyurl.com/34jmn7tp. Accessed on 17 October 2025.

Afterword

When Avishkar decided to join the family business, it brought me a deep sense of satisfaction and calm. What mattered most to me was not the decision itself, but the manner in which he arrived at it. He did not rush. He observed, learned and reflected before choosing his path. This made his decision both meaningful and mature.

A family business is not merely about continuity; it is about responsibility. It carries years of effort, struggle and values passed down from one generation to the next. When a young person enters such a business by choice—and not by pressure—it reflects commitment and respect for that legacy.

After Avishkar joined, I felt reassured. He came with humility, patience and a genuine desire to understand the people and systems before introducing change. As a father, this gave me confidence that the foundation we built would be handled with care. As a professional, it gave me hope that the business would evolve with time while remaining rooted in its core values.

It is a wise choice when the next generation takes time, gains perspective and then decides to contribute with sincerity. Avishkar's journey reflects this balance between learning from the past and preparing for the future. I believe this book captures these realities honestly and will be helpful to many families walking a similar path.

—Pramod Kumar Srivastava
Group Director and CEO, The PDP Group®

Acknowledgements

Writing this book would have been impossible without the support of my parents—Mr Pramod Kumar Srivastava and Mrs Rupa Srivastava—who, besides giving me so much love and support, have spent over three decades of their married life taking our family business to the level where it is today. Thank you for everything.

I would like to thank my wife, Srayasi, who was my girlfriend and fiancée for almost the entire time I wrote this book. Your support and unwavering belief in me made this journey possible.

I am grateful to my sister, Divya, whose lifelong love of books encouraged me to develop reading as a habit. Although I never really took to fiction as a teenager, her passion for reading eventually inspired me to develop an interest in non-fiction in my twenties.

I want to thank my relatives, who always encourage me to aim higher and take the family business to greater heights. As a youngster in the family business, I maintain both personal and professional relationships with some of my relatives, and they have always supported me in carving my own path.

I am also grateful to all my office colleagues at 'The PDP Group®', whom we proudly refer to as PDPians. They inspire me each day with their consistency and hard work. It is their support and good wishes that have enabled us to have sustained growth over the years.

I am grateful to my school, South Point, Kolkata, for teaching me the importance of staying calm under pressure; to my junior college, Christ Junior College, Bangalore, for giving me exposure to a new academic environment and helping me make lifelong friends, and to my universities—the University of Auckland, New Zealand (where I spent 3 years), and the University of Nottingham (where I spent a semester)—for grounding me further and teaching me to focus on *how* to think rather than *what* to think.

I would like to thank professional associations such as National Association of Container Freight Stations (NACFS), Business Network International (BNI), International Federation of Freight Forwarders Associations (FIATA), Association of Multimodal Transport Operators of India (AMTOI) and Federation of Freight Forwarders' Associations in India (FFFAI), which provide young business professionals with a platform to express their views and to develop their public speaking and networking skills.

Finally, I would like to thank my friends, acquaintances and those who may no longer be in touch but have left a lasting impact on shaping who I am today.